Light
and
Shadows

Herbert Windolf

**Publications by Herbert Windolf,
As Translator of Karl May**

Published by Washington State University Press:
The Oil Prince

Published through BookSurge:
Black Mustang
with Marlies Bugman

Published by Nemsi Books:
The Treasure of Silver Lake
The Ghost of Llano Estacado
The Son of the Bear Hunter
Imaginary Journeys I
Imaginary Journeys II
Imaginary Journeys III
Thoughts of Heaven
Winnetou IV
Pacific Shores
The Inca's Legacy
The Scout
Deadly Dust
The Mahdi I

Published through CreateSpace:
The Mahdi II
The Mahdi III
One More Day . . .
As Translator of Autobiography of Isabell Steiner

As Author of Poetic Prose:
Through Booksurge:
Observations and Reflections
Pondering What Is
Otherwise
Musings
Contemplations
Through Kindle Direct Publishing:
Thoughts
Searching
Shadows and Light

Private Printing:
Biography – Bridges Across Times and Continents

Published by Verlag für Tiefenpsychologie und Anthropologie:
Brücken über Zeiten und Kontinente,
Biography – with Dorothea Rutkowsky

Planetary Studies Foundation Quarterly
Travelogues:
A Hike in Provence
A Safari Through Namibia
Alaska, the Last Terrestrial Frontier of the US
Galápagos
Excursions in Saxony's Switzerland
Monumental Sights, in Grand Staircase/Escalante, Utah, and
Northernmost Arizona
Journey to Sumatra
Zambezi
Moroccan Impressions
The Lure of Africa
Tanzania Redux, unpublished

Planetary Studies Foundation Quarterly
Ten Explorations, six published:
The likely Futility of S.E.T.I. Programs
Snowball Earth
Wondrous Water
The Probability for Intelligent Life in the Universe
A Personal View of Existentialism
Tsunami
Pragmatism
Forty billion Potentially Habitable Planets
Exceptionalism
December 26, 1776

Annemarie Schnitt - Willkommen Website
Translations of Poems and Stories

Unpublished – for Private Use
Autobiography
Translations:
The Texas War of Independence in 1836
by Herman Ehrenberg
Five Years Behind Barbed Wire
by Walter Hartmann
Letters to David Walter
Heinrich Himmler, by Franz Wegener
Ukraine Letters, by Hans Windolf
Germany's Final Months of WWII, Diary of Hans Windolf
The Forgotten Generation, by Sabine Bode
War's Grandchildren, by Sabine Bode
Genesis, by Dorothea Rutkowsky

Courses facilitated:
From the Spice Trade to Globalization
Cataclysms and Extinctions
The Likely Futility of SETI Programs
The Cambrian Explosion
Human Evolution and Migration
The American National Mind vis-à-vis the Rest of the World

Addendum
in Thoughts
A Collection of Haiku Verses

Addendum
in Searching
Three African Stories

Addendum
in Shadows and Light
Ten Explorations

Table of Contents: **Page:**

Table of Contents: **Page:**

Table of Contents: **Page:**

Table of Contents: **Page:**

Table of Contents: **Page:**

Table of Contents: **Page:**

Ten Explorations

Introduction

Was it prescient that I chose the title of this volume, *Shadows and Light*, before the calamity of the Covid-19 pandemic struck in the middle of my eighth collection of comments on life? For plenty of shadows, SARS-CoV-2 – the name of the virus – has brought to the world which cannot help but be changed. At present, the politicians of the many nations of the world do not cooperate. Everyone is concerned with their own troubles, the *Shadows*, this virus has brought. It can only be hoped – it is a must – that world leaders will come together, including, in particular, a responsible leader of the United States of America, to help create a new world of *Light,* as happened after WWII.

I hope that by the time I am able to publish this volume, the troubles I addressed will have become history. If not, ours will be a rather shadowy planet.

On a personal level – I cannot claim wisdom for it – I saw the calamity coming, health-wise and economically, before the experts did, I prepared for a four-month isolation for the purpose of "breaking the chain" of transmission, and to "flatten the curve," to stretch out the time and facilities of the soon to be sorely taxed, medical personnel and facilities. This was in my own interest and that of the community. I made a list of items I thought necessary to "survive" for an extended period of time and did my shopping a week before the run on supplies started. Oddly, and amusingly, the supply of toilet paper was cleaned out everywhere. Even now, four weeks after the pandemic was declared, the shelves for toilet paper are empty. People must be full of it. I have psycho-analyzed American society and think it must still be in the Freudian Anal Stage.

Eventually, no later than August/September of this year 2020, I will need to "surface," join the world again and paint the town. At this point, it is likely that I, too, will become infected. Maybe it will be moderate; maybe it will be severe. But by that time I hope that our medical system is operating again on a more normal level.

At present, I feel my health is passable. Menière's vertigo is in remission, and my hemolytic anemia is stable. However, my eyesight gives me trouble as well as my left knee. If worse comes to worst, I may yet have to bite the sour apple of a knee replacement, once the pandemic has abated. But who knows? If all goes well, I hope to observe the foibles of our species for a few more years. By that time I will be almost 84 years old. It should be very interesting, and en*light*ening.

In the meantime, the streets of Prescott are mostly empty. The people of this city largely abide by the order of staying home and not socializing. I paid my house cleaner for a few months of not cleaning. We can still meet outside our homes at a distance of six feet. It is interesting how friends now relate to each other. Some call and/or email on a regular basis. Others seem to brood. Some use Chat systems. Others take daily walks. Many clean house. I have suggested that they can always start at the beginning again if the isolation continues.

As of Tuesday, April 7, I will enter, what I call "enhanced isolation." Until now I have minimized my city exposure to doctors' visits and light shopping. At times I also pick up items for friends. However, in the future this will be restricted to a week or ten day intervals. Afternoons I am usually asked by my RikkiCat to accompany her outside onto the deck or to the yard. There, I sit on one of my many boulders while she explores the neighborhood or sits next to me. Problems with my knee limit my walking and gymnastics. Mornings I record whatever I can find of decent or semi-decent TV shows to view later. If my deteriorating eyesight were better, I would love to read more. As it is, I am only able to read for a short time.

If a future reader of these lines by chance happens to come across a copy of this booklet, I hope he or she will find my account of the mundane events of this trying time of interest. But then I hope the pandemic will have long been left behind. May there be brighter times ahead.

Globalization, already in trouble before this calamity, has come to a screeching halt. Travel in all forms has dwindled to a minimum. Airlines have reduced flights, and staff clamor for financial help from governments. China, South Korea, and Taiwan have pulled out from the downturn, and are almost back to normal. But who will buy their products with Western countries in the doldrums? Their internal purchasing power will not suffice to keep their economies humming.

When societies become troubled because of societal or economic discrepancies, there appears to be a rise in authoritarian regimes. Examples are the long established Russian and Chinese governments, but newer ones include the Philippines under Duerte, Hungary under Orban, Poland under Kaszinsky, Brazil under Bolsonaro, and, unavoidably, I must include, the United States of America under Trump. The United Kingdom is riven by its Brexit uncertainties. What other authoritarian regimes may yet come into being in the wake of the Covid-19 crisis?

The tendency toward authoritarianism precedes Covid-19 and has been caused by the negative effects of globalization which, by itself, has brought unprecedented well-being to hundreds of thousands of human beings while simultaneously disenfranchised groups in other societies. The increased movement of people across geographic distances made possible by new technology and transportation further aggravates the pressure on established political entities in the West, Europe and the USA, and the Pacific region, Australia and New Zealand. More and more, these pressures increase the trend of political entities to look out for their own interest, forging ever poorer cooperation across political borders. However, this pandemic has shown that such cooperation is precisely what is called for. Let us hope that, when the dust has settled, leaders will locate a place to convene a gathering of nations like after WWII to agree on ways to live successfully together for decades to come. May a bright light shine through for all of us to come together.

Once more, I thank my wife Ute for making the cover image available, and my editors, Lynn Chesson and Zene Krogh, for their diligence in correcting my mistakes. Whatever mistakes are left are mine.

Almost three months have passed since I wrote the above lines. My eighth book is ready to be formatted and published once the final editing and proof-reading are done.

The experience of these three months has been sobering, for the world and for me. In Western democratic countries, with their less disciplined and freedom-oriented societies, it is difficult to maintain social distancing and isolation. I speak in the present tense because this problem continues and is aggravating the infectious situation. June, and shortly July, will see an increase in infections across wide swaths of the country. There are many hot-spots in U.S. and European cities.

The fatalities in the U.S. at the end of June 2020 stand at 124,000 and approach 500,000 worldwide, and are still climbing. Much of this is due to people needing freedom, some of it powered by ideology, but most by personal need.

For me, I have discovered what a social creature I am needing physical contact with friends and family. Email and phone calls are just not enough. There is the desire to have lunch or dinner with friends, either at homes, but preferably going out to restaurants which are slowly opening with spaced seating. Take-outs are okay but simply don't cut it because the ambiance is lacking.

It is interesting how friends, and the wider population, are dealing with the perceived danger of infection. I have likened the perception of risk by this population with that of smokers: "I get my pleasure now. The future be damned." Another perspective is likely that the climbing death rate seems distant, removed from everyday life, even though there's frequent reporting and exhortation in the news on how to behave. The perception is that the increase in the number of deaths is happening to others, and is not close to home.

Some people go for walks, sometimes with friends. Others, with a tendency to be recluses have become more so. A few are prepared to meet with friends on a one-on-one basis for a meal, preferably outdoors. Others feel it's too risky to meet. Several even barely communicate by phone or email. Chacun à son goût, as my deceased, now three years gone friend, would have said, who is missing it all.

The remedy of a vaccine is likely but still at least a year away. How will people deal with a time span twice as long as we have so far endured? The acceptance of attrition will grow and people will go their ways. May we see a bright light once more in the future, a future which will probably be different from recent decades but, hopefully, better for all.

Prescott, AZ   Herbert Windolf

Shadows and Light

Try, we should, to always rise
from the shadows to the light.
As hard as it sometimes seems to be
we have the power to overcome,
the power of spirit
to become more than we appear.
If we have will and conquer fear.

If you plan on being anything less than you are capable of
being,
you will probably be unhappy all the days of your life.
Abraham Maslow

Wondering

May not only your head be turned
by my cover of Shadows and Light,
but, here and there
your wondering mind.

When one door closes, another opens.
Or you can open the closed door.
That's how doors work.
Unknown

Integrity, once more

Being honest and morally upright
to others and more so, oneself.
Being whole and undivided,
of clear and rational sense
is integrity, hence.

You have exactly one life in which to do
everything you'll ever do.
Act accordingly.
Colin Wright

3

Babble

Think clearly. Write clearly. Talk clearly.
Have something worthwhile to say.
Don't be greedy hearing yourself.
Observe the reaction of listeners.
Truly listen to what's being said.
Do not interrupt.
Evaluate what's being said.
Respond in a measured way.
Ask questions, don't reject.
Integrate what's new.
Don't be defensive.
Learn!
Don't babble.

Be careful with your words.
Once they are said, they can only be forgiven,
not forgotten.
Unknown

Lost Friends

What does a schnorrer,
a Trump-voter, a creationist,
and a babbler have in common?
None has integrity, none makes sense.
The schnorrer takes but doesn't give.
The voter sullies his integrity
by supporting his idol's lack thereof.
The creationist is plain silly,
picking what he likes or needs,
and all too often denies
human-caused global warming
threatening a viable society.
And a babbler deals in trivialities.
Good riddance all.

Sometimes you have to give up on people.
Not because you don't care, but because they don't.
Miss Sunshine

Stories

For thousands of years
we've concocted stories,
stories of what life is supposed to be.
When, oh when, will we devise a story
which will help us the world
to properly see?

What screws us up most in life
is the picture in our head of how it is supposed to be.
Unknown

Volition

The power of using one's will.
To decide among different choices.

I'm not telling you it is going to be easy,
I'm telling you it's going to be worth it.
Weight loss Motivation

Reflections

The fire is burning lower.
Embers glow in the dark.
Thoughts arise of what all I've committed,
and where I've left my mark.
Where I have failed,
what I have learned,
where I've succeeded,
where I got burned.
There's the age-old thought:
"If only I could go back,
and right the wrongs
for a better track."
But as it happens,
without mistakes,
we wouldn't learn,
belatedly,
what it truly takes.

Welcome to the Karma Cafe.
There are no menus,
you will get served what you deserve.
Unknown

Enough is Enough

New afflictions keep popping up.
After cataract surgery
neither with nor without glasses is my vision clear.
Wet macular degeneration now impairs my left eye.
An MRI is needed for the left knee,
following my fall three months ago.
For this my pacemaker needs to be put to sleep.
Thus, my wife Ute asked me
for when she will drive me
to the hospital's MRI facility:
"What should I do if your heart suddenly stops?"
"Let me go," I said. "No further prop."
I'm tired of all these afflictions popping up.
Might I, however, yet be given the gift of some years
not by ailments constantly riven,
what joy it would be, ha,
an unimpaired living.

Our temperament
decides the value of everything brought to us by fortune.
François de La Rochefoucauld

9

Reckoning

It has come to pass
that we reckon today
by the Gregorian calendar,
time passed since the presumed
birth of Christ.
What happened before is called BC,
Before Christ,
what happened after is AD,
Anno Domini,
the Year of the Lord.
Since many cultures don't recognize this Lord,
instead of AD we worldwide use CE,
for Common Era,
and BCE
Before the Common Era.

What you choose also chooses you.
Kamand Kojouri

Unity

True unity of our being
calls for reason
to check our feeling.
Yet feeling, emotion, also powers reason,
lies at the root of what we call mind.
The seat of "heart" and reason combined.

You cannot be truly humble, unless you truly believe
that life can and will go on without you.
Mokokoma Mokhonoana

Indictment

What is one to make of the ethics
of a creature, a man,
who cheats, lies, abrogates, backstabs,
demeans, abandons, contradicts himself, is vindictive,
and yet is supported by many a woman and man?
But rather the question is:
What is one to make of the voters
holding to him?
If they support such non-ethical behavior,
does this not reflect on them?
Are they not guilty of the same lack of ethics,
the same mayhem?

Wear none of thine own chains; but keep free,
whilst thou art free.
William Penn

12

Duality

The moment existence came into being,
the creation of galaxies and stars.
Once the sun shone brightly,
life and death came into being,
duality was born.

What keeps us alive?
Fear that we might not be.
Ljupka Cvetanova

LUCA

Last Universal Common Ancestor
going back four billion years,
from which all life has sprung,
it appears.
But since "universal" and "common"
mean more or less the same,
a more succinct acronym is LUA,
our Last Common Ancestor
of whom we are heirs.

The unspoken rule of democracy:
three stupid ones will always outvote two smart ones.
Ljupka Cvetanova

Understanding

As age creeps up at different rates
understanding what's being said gets ever worse.
Three things we oldsters need keep in mind:
Is it our loss of hearing that makes us blind?
Is it that our fading ability
to process spoken information
is putting us into a bind?
Or, what is worse,
are we projecting from our mind
what we think is being said,
but aren't truly listening to what's outlined.
Thus, get hearing aids of some kind;
ask your partner to slow down his speech,
and/or repeat;
and most important, don't neglect,
keep your mouth shut, listen attentively,
don't project.

Patriotism is the narcissism of countries.
Mokokoma Mokhonoana

Consciousness,

---

gift of the gods, or the devil's, maybe?
no, rather evolved, through Nature's creativity.
Like other beings dim at first,
grown to the present through millions of years.
That we can ponder why we are here,
what might be our purpose, if any there be.
Dream up stories how life ought to be lived.
But nagging is our knowledge that we must die,
lose our precious consciousness,
life's meaning, becoming dust, such distress!
No longer see the blue of sky,
talk to a pet, or with a friend,
enjoy food, still take a trip,
at times enjoy a pleasant nip.
Soon see a doctor every week, in a hospice vegetate,
there for a final breath to wait.

Recurring in old poems it is said:
Timor mortis conturbat me.
Yet I say:
I am not afraid because I understand.

Processing

One other capacity that's slipping away
is the processing of verbal information
coming my way.
And I know of a friend, worse off that I,
who no longer is able to make hay.
There's the need to ask a partner to slow down,
to repeat what's been said,
without looking the clown.
Or worse, having lost one's marbles
which once were one's very own.
A TV science program turning to dross,
when I'm unable to follow its discourse.
Written information becoming a pain.
The mental desire to tell the writer:
"Don't bore me with details;
hurry up, say what you mean!"

Often enough to get past the chaff
I only read an article's last paragraph.
And what is it with a friend of mine
who, instead of the earlier six weeks,
now wants every two weeks to meet?
Has he lost his sense of time?
Where are we headed in our decline?

Loneliness tortures many if not most of the elderly
more intensely and more frequently than it torments many,
if not most of us who will never be
or have not yet been pushed or pulled into old age.
Mokokoma Mokhonoana

18

Boulders 1

My yard holds many boulders.
Five in the back are just right to sit.
Weather permitting, almost every day,
twice, if possible, I go out of my way,
to sit on one, either in sunshine or shade,
when RikkiCat asks for my company there.
Alert she is, having met other critters,
javelina, a bobcat, and deer.
My presence provides security
keeping the area all clear.

In searching for myself,
I have created myself.
Ljupka Cvetanova

19

Cats vs. Dogs

Dogs take their masters for a walk.
For an open door is all cats ask.
Dogs are a nuisance when they bark.
Cats use their repertoire to talk.

I saw an injured black cat.
God knows, who has crossed her path.
Ljupka Cvetanova

Proactive

He or she who creates or controls situations
before they are to happen is proactive
rather than the one responding
to when they have already taken place.
There are two kinds of people,
the former rare,
the latter humankind's majority,
to say so being not unfair.

Children are our future.
Unfortunately, we are their past.
Ljupka Cvetanova

21

Hope

With all the turmoil we hear of every day
it's easy to imagine humanity fail.
But if we look back thousands,
ten thousands of years,
we find fights, killings, mayhem,
being the rule of the day,
interrupted by peaceful existence,
as it may.
Crude behavior was dominant,
ethics undeveloped, poor.
Then, despite today's turmoil
we must admit:
"We have come a long way."

Never deprive someone of hope –
it may be all they have.
Unknown

Habits

We all follow behavioral patterns,
ingrained, some benign.
When the time arises to make a change,
it's not easy to follow a new design.
Aware we must be of what we do,
then make the decision
to change for the new.
It isn't easy to succeed as planned,
but takes awareness and decision
going hand in hand.

It is as common for tastes to change
as it is uncommon for traits of character.
François de La Rochefoucauld

23

Concoctions 1

Gods are a-dime-a-dozen,
sprung from the human mind.
And spiritual mumbo-jumbo
is not far behind.
Nature simply is, doesn't give a damn.
But mankind needs solace,
thus concocts plenty a scam.
Do live a full life
for as long as you can,
and, as little as possible,
don't hurt anyone.

Whenever a theory appears to you as the only possible one,
take this as a sign that you have neither understood the
theory
nor the problem which it was intended to solve.
Karl Popper

The Fire

---

burns lower.
Embers still glow.
At times yet a spark flies,
that's as far as it goes.

How do I know what I think
till I have written it down.
Dorian Rolston

Innocence

There is this story of the Garden of Eden,
where the first human beings lived,
innocent, like animals,
not knowing the difference
between good and bad.
Then, when we ate
from the Apple of Knowledge,
when we became conscious,
the world forever changed.
I am no believer of stories,
but this one is as good as it gets.

Good tests kill flawed theories;
we remain alive to guess again.
Karl Popper

Light 1

These days, my eyesight fading,
I need as much light as I can get.
The best is at my desk facing west.
It doesn't take long for Rikki to jump up,
and plunk herself before me to rest.
While I read, I can caress her at times.
She seems to enjoy it,
then, too, the pleasure is mine.
What might she be thinking
while I whisper in her ear?
Might the feeling of love
and being loved
also a gift given her?

Horror is the law of the world of living creatures,
and civilization is concerned with masking the truth.
Czeslaw Milosz

27

Testimonials

As I've said a while ago,
I first and foremost write for myself.
Some poems help me crystallize thoughts
dwelling half-resolved,
some are memories of a long gone day,
occasionally there's even a jest, yippy yay.
Yet I also salve my precious ego,
by telling others in my publications
what I think of my world,
and what they ought and ought not to do.
Not that I expect my books
rapidly disappearing from shelves.
It is thus a pleasure, rare as it is,
to receive a testimonial about my prosaic ideas.

The purpose of poetry is to remind us
how difficult it is to remain just one person,
for our house is open, there are no keys in the doors,
and invisible guests come in and out at will.
Czeslaw Milosz

Wordplay

At doctors' offices it has come to pass
that for identification your birthdate is routinely asked.
Upon confirming it, I can't help but slip in
"No change yet."
Entering a store, a sales person asking
"Can I help you?"
I retort
"I'm afraid I can't be helped."
which usually results in a pleasant exchange.
When I called a lady friend to stop by in the morn,
told "I'm not yet dressed,
"Give me fifteen minutes,"
my response was, I confess,
"Don't you worry.
I'll take you dressed or undressed."
One needs to know when what can be said,
if it results in a laugh its aim has been met.

All bad poetry springs from genuine feeling.
Oscar Wilde

Wordsmith

Arriving in Canada in nineteen-sixty-four,
I was quite proficient in English, I thought.
But then I found out, felt like a fish out of water,
that my English in no way matched my German power.
It took many years for my vocabulary to grow,
to learn the idioms, the prepositions,
and what else of American culture was to know.
Fifty-five years later, I am happy to say,
"My command of the American language
surpasses my German of earlier days,
and, what's more, is more fun with to play."
Many an American word, spelled differently,
when spoken has a different meaning.
Oh, what a joy it is to allude,
to tease, to cause a smile, on my fellow-beings' faces
or, better yet, to have a good laugh.

You see how I try – To reach with words –
What matters most – And how I fail.
Czeslaw Milosz

Profundity

Having written now in excess of 1400 poems,
or rather Poetic Prose,
I've run out of profound things to say,
and deal increasingly with earthy subjects,
more akin to straw and hay.
But it's still fun to rhyme a bit, to compose,
and perhaps, here and there,
say something less profound,
but rather a bit loose.
And it keeps my mind hustling
instead of rusting.

To be what we are,
and to become what we are capable of becoming,
is the only end of life.
Robert Louis Stevenson

Wildness

Tens of thousands of years ago
wolves, being pack animals, like us,
domesticated themselves to become dogs.
To hunt with, to cuddle, to guide,
to be show animals, their owners pride.
Last not least, to take their masters out
for a walk and for them to pick up
what they leave behind.
At most ten thousand years in the past
cats attached themselves, hunting rats and mice.
Solitary and independent they were and still are,
some have been tamed, their breeds also named.
Yet the bush, the savannah, the jungle,
is still not far when looking at a tabby,
not an exhibition star.

There are times when my RikkiCat and I
face each other eye-to-eye
that the wildness of her species
can still stare at me with a fierceness,
teeth and claws always ready to strike.
From a dog's look a far cry.

Everything comes to us from others.
To be is to belong to someone.
Jean Paul Sartre

Stoicism

What cannot be changed
must be endured.
Only that which can be challenged and changed,
for which solutions can be found,
can be attuned.
And while I have described
my trials and tribulations
in some of my poems,
through the past two years,
I've tried to deal with them, endure them,
without shedding tears.
It makes me a kind of stoic, it appears.
On the whole, I suppose,
what I can't change I let be.
At times I can bitch about it,
that's for sure.

Where we have an emotional stake in an idea,
we are most likely to deceive ourselves.
Carl Sagan

Democracy

One problem with democracy is, I maintain,
all too often,
people vote their gut,
emotion,
not their brain.

Democracy is also a form of worship.
It is the worship of jackals by jackasses.
H. L. Mencken

Parsimony

To be thrifty,
be economic in the use of means to an end.
William of Ockham, in what today is called
Occam's Razor,
proposed this rule, which I'd like to amend.
More and more I do away with superfluous words,
cut to the chase,
come to the point,
to say what I mean.

I was working on the proof of one of my poems all the
morning,
and took out a comma. In the afternoon I put it back again.
Oscar Wilde

Shadows 1

Shadow persists where there's no light.
Darkness engenders fear,
by which we abide.
Hence it's our task
to illuminate the mind.

It is even harder for the average ape
to believe that he has descended from man.
H.L. Mencken

Liberally vs Conservatively

To a meeting of Democrats at a restaurant
I was invited.
At Happy Hour it was to be.
My hosts suggested to drink liberally.
My retort was
"The last time at this place
I had two margaritas
and enchiladas with beans and rice.
For this, I paid twice.
Should I drink conservatively,
Would that be just as nice?"

Half the work that is done in the world
is to make things appear what they are not.
E. R. Beadle

Contributions

Behold, reading the following:
I am a wannabe anthropologist.
There is only one species, no races,
only ethnic differences.
At root, we are the same. –
Sixty years ago, in nineteen sixty one,
I became friends in Paris,
at the Alliance Française, with Tony Soon Ho,
Chinese from Singapore.
Later, staying at my home,
we discussed the merits and demerits
of Europe and China,
which had contributed what, and which had done more.

While I recognized the great contributions
of Chinese culture,
I claimed what no other people before had done,
that Europeans, for better or worse,
had made the world one.

Success is dependent on effort.
Sophocles.
Also on greed, and reaching beyond one's doors.
H.W.

40

Thought

My last poem in "Searching"
I called "Sui Generis."
Few will know this Latin term,
and fewer will look it up to learn.
Words, which make language,
give meaning to thought.
Without definitions our thoughts remain naught,
a melange of emotions forever unwrought.
Communication in a language can be conducted
with a few hundred words,
and some grammatical rules, is all it takes.
But the power of words,
so as not impoverished to remain,
opens a world as never before.
Living this world enriches, makes our lives,
which is why we ought to know
as many words as we can derive.

Words have no power to impress the mind
without the exquisite horror of their reality.
Edgar Allan Poe

Burden

There's a friend who thinks
being educated a burden,
and thinking of the unwashed masses
being a collection of uneducated asses.
While this stance contains
a rather large kernel of truth,
I beg to disagree, it being not entirely sooth.
There is many a pearl shining bright in the dark,
and there are many more, unbeknownst,
if I may so remark.
I, myself, journey outside this arc.

A bridge has no allegiance to either side.
Les Coleman

Aliens

There was this guy from funky Sedona
who seriously claimed
there be aliens on Earth.
I thought him nuts
and let him be.
These days, though, when I see
some of these made-up faces,
the contorted visages, the stiff Melania, on TV,
I can't help but wonder
whether this fellow hadn't lost all his marbles,
and trumped us unbelievers,
whoopee!

People are to be taken in very small doses.
Ralph Waldo Emerson

43

Covid-19

---

its virus originator called SARS-CoV-2,
will be the worst pandemic
the world has seen.
Mind you, the world will also survive,
but much will change in people's behavior
and globalization will take a dive.
It will not be possible to prevent its spread,
for the Third World it will become a dread.
Plenty of people are bound to die,
especially those over eighty, like me.
But I've taken my measures to survive.
When it is time, I will isolate myself
and say: let's wait and see.
And should I be wrong in my assumptions,
there's always a new day.

You see how I try
To reach with words
What matters most
And how I fail.
Czeslaw Milosz.

44

Technophobe

It has come to pass
that I care less and less
for the evermore complex techno-mess.
Boeing planes fall from the sky,
computer systems go awry,
spam and hackers multiply.
Software's impenetrable, but not for malware.
Power fails us, here and there.
Cars get recalled by the millions.
Smart-phones, smart-phones everywhere.
I don't want one, heaven beware.

Beware lest you lose the substance by grasping at the
shadow.
Aesop

Projecting

Speak firmly, don't prattle, enunciate,
project your persona for proper effect.
This doesn't mean to neglect
the old adage to
speak softly but carry a big stick.

One can choose to go back toward safety
or forward toward growth.
Growth must be chosen again and again;
fear must be overcome again and again.
Abraham Maslow

Empiricism

We groped our way
from ignorance and superstition
to the genesis of empiricism,
the process of verifiable observation.
We owe ancient Greek philosophers
the initial broad exploration of our world,
mostly attempted by theory and logic.
After only a few hundred years of empiricism
we still have a long way to go,
to become Homo sapiens from Homo perturbatio
and leave thinking by beliefs behind.

It is folly for a man to pray to the gods
for that which he has the power to obtain by himself.
Epicurus

Boulders 2

My backyard holds several boulders
just right for sitting on.
In the course of the day
some are in shade,
some in the warmth of the sun.
For twenty-seven years I have lived
with this bouldered yard,
and only now at eighty-three
have discovered the pleasure of this part.

I don't think of the misery, but of all the beauty that remains.
Anne Frank

Washing Hands

In a poem a decade ago
I urged people to give this activity a go.
Now, with Covid-19 an ever present woe,
to thoroughly wash hands
is recommended left and right by the pros.
Yet, not one of these experts I've seen on TV
rubbed their fingers in between,
the thumbs, the tips, the nails.
Well, then, that's where no viruses grow?
So much for this highly recommended
treatment against Covid-19!

If parents could only realize
how they bore their children.
George Bernard Shaw

Or pundits
H.W.

Civilizations

Twelve thousand years ago the last ice age faded.
Then it took five thousand years
for civilizations, the first city states,
at various locations around the globe, to rise.
Tribes agglomerated and invented
beliefs and creation stories.
States came into being,
a global connection evolved.
How will it continue?
To ever larger social constructs, or
an eventual collapse, a
devolution into tribal groups?

Nothing lasts forever.
H.W.

Observer

No way can I say
that I am the ultimate observer.
Too many things go by the wayside.
But when I observe
how many people stumble through life,
not catching what's happening under their eyes,
I cannot help but think that I am doing alright.
Not everyone can be a Michel de Montaigne.

When dealing with the insane,
the best method is to pretend to be sane.
Hermann Hesse

Prosetry

Allow me, literary world,
to coin a term for what I write.
I've called my scribbles poetic prose.
Prosetry would do, I suppose.

Friends

My friends are dwindling.
Some are gone.
With others I'm done.
Those that are left,
some younger, some older,
are succumbing to what age is holding.
I still do quite well,
physically and mentally,
but I observe the creep,
detestable both,
yet no sense to weep.

Forgiveness is not an emotion, it's a decision.
Randall Worley

Vivid

Lately, I'm haunted by vivid dreams,
nothing exceptional, just mundane scenes.
One, where I do my business standing up.
Drowsily, I realize I'm still in the sack.
Then fully awake and quite afraid,
I frantically check
whether I wetted my bed.

Calm down. Both your sins and good deeds
will be lost in oblivion.
Czeslaw Milosz

Fez

Ancient city of human life.
I remember you well,
your narrow passages and aisles,
to their left and right these marvelous sights.
Never losing sight of our guide,
for on your own, you'd never again
see the outside light.
The vendors perched behind their stalls
selling to the world for whatever it calls.
The butchers, a camel head displayed,
the bakers, their flatbread, their delicacies on hand.
The fruits and veggies, some exotic, some known,
the barbers, the weavers, shoemakers, and more.
All the while, one must be on one's toes
when a donkey heavily loaded
needs the right of way,
everyone stepping out of its sway.
Oh, and the spices, their colors, their scents,
and somewhere the odor where leather is cured,
where the visitor is handed a twig of peppermint.

Women shopping with covered heads,
a few emancipated show their faces.
The time then comes for a little repast
for which the guide takes you to
what looks like a hole in the ground,
but by no means mean.
Clean it is, delicious the food,
slow-cooked in a ceramic tagine.
Once more ambling through the warren of aisles,
you wonder what all has gone on and still does
behind the ancient walls to the left and right.

Imposition

Never did I impose myself on a woman.
I have wondered why?
Was I simply too shy?
Or was it respect that kept me at bay?
Was it that I grew up with three strong women,
without grandfathers, a father faraway?

Success is achieved by developing our strength,
not by eliminating our weaknesses.
Marilyn vos Savant

Exercise

It is a drag.
Many love it,
but I don't brag,
saying if only
I could do without.
Yet there's always
this haunting nag.
Because without
I'd likely be earlier dead.

Strength does not come from physical capacity.
It comes from an indomitable will.
Mahatma Gandhi

Bucket List

I never had a bucket list
just did what came to mind.
I never cared for crowded places,
but more for the solitary kind.
Having seen quite a few parts of this world,
I loved most what I saw.
But age and health have now put a limit
on what I still could draw.
Surprise, I now have a bucket list,
but thimble-size it is,
and fantasy, more than less.
It is the Marquesas cruise,
three years ago, I left behind.
But at the top of this little thimble
there's always another African safari,
a canoe trip down the Zambezi river,
I'm sure the elephants and hippos wouldn't mind.

Age is strictly a case of mind over matter.
If you don't mind it doesn't matter.
Jack Benny

Speaking Out

There are people who carry a hurt.
Others are angry,
others too timid,
others confused,
some are abused.
Some lack the will
to speak out,
keep what's bothering them at bay.
And then there are those
who have nothing to say.

How do I know what I think till I have written it down!
Oswald Veblen.

Depression

I cannot help but think
that many a depression
is the manifestation of a need unfulfilled,
most subconscious, few accessible to will.

Being defeated is often a temporary condition.
Giving up is what makes it permanent.
Marilyn vos Savant

Delight

What pleasure it is to watch
feathery clouds drift slowly
in front of a mountain ridge.
At dusk they tend to descend
into a valley at hand,
only to rise in the young day,
drawn by the sun's warming rays.
And what a delight it is to see
mountain tops protruding from a sea
of clouds, as if there were nothing beneath.

All pleasures are commendable that do not culminate in
regret.
Françoise d' Aubigne Marquise de Maintenon

Loki

My psycho-friend Norm
honored me today
by applying a, what he thought appropriate,
nickname to me,
Loki,
the Trickster god of Norse mythology.
That's as close as I come, god-like to be.
Norm thinks that I'm playing this game,
twisting and teasing without shame.
Come to think, I realize now,
why I am fond of the coyote,
the Indian trickster of fame.
Ah, why not have a little fun in life
and proudly carry Loki's name.
Yet, I need to watch out,
Loki ended when to a rock he was bound.

The trouble with man is twofold.
He cannot learn truths which are too complicated;
he forgets truths which are too simple.
Rebecca West

Marriage

It just occurred to me
how close two beings can come to be,
how they interact, how they relate,
how they talk to each other,
how they behave.
Should you think I'm talking
about husband and wife,
you are mistaken.
I'm referring here to my cat Rikki
and myself.
But what a traumatic experience for her it would be,
if or when this creature will survive me.

With the fortunate everything is fortunate.
Horace

Michel de Montaigne

---

once more comes to mind,
when he suggested that he wrote
of daily life's occurrences,
the ordinary kind.
Often such simple stories contain
an insight, a subtle allusion.
Sometimes, when nothing else comes to mind,
I'm not averse to leaving simple things behind.

God made everything out of nothing,
but the nothingness shows through.
Paul Valery

Challenges

If there is something of the past I regret
it's that not more intelligent people I've met
to probe and explore, to challenge my intellect.
Gosh, what opportunities I missed,
now that life's end is in sight,
but at the tunnel's end,
there's still some light.
In the meantime, though,
I can caress my cat while I write,
next to the computer.
A most pleasing delight.

Fear vs Concern

Fear is emotional,
prudent is concern.
Fear is born of ignorance,
concern of rational thought.
Fear gives rise to irrational action,
initiative results from concern.
And if this isn't enough of a worry,
fear is visceral, expecting harm.
Angst is lingering anxiety,
apprehension, even doom.

Be able to notice all the confusion between fact
and opinion that appears in the news.
Marilyn vos Savant

Twitchings

My cat twitching her tail,
and a man – short of one –
twitching his knee,
have a neurophysical effect in common.
Neither possesses the awareness to leave it be.

Do not fear to be eccentric in opinion,
for every opinion now accepted was once eccentric.
Bertrand Russell

Narcissism

There was this boy, Narcissus by name,
who fell in love with himself in the water's reflection.
Unable to acquire his object of desire,
he couldn't help but to expire.
In a person we call this vanity,
selfishness, a sense of entitlement,
a need for admiration, a lack of empathy.
When people fly their country's flag excessively,
can this then be called national narcissism?

Do not spoil what you have by desiring what you have not;
remember that what you now have was once
among the things you only hoped for.
Epicurus

Dinner

Tonight I was invited to a dinner of four,
in 2020 the fifteenth of March.
The Lithuanian stew and Georgian wine were tasty,
the conversation about Covid-19 and its effects
was vivid, noisy, at times a roar.
I couldn't help pointing this out to the three,
or should I include the observer, us four?

Fear makes us feel our humanity.
Benjamin Disraeli

When It Counts

As mentioned before,
I kid a lot,
and Loki's now my name.
Many times I've told my friends:
"Don't believe all that I say.
Only when it counts."

Beauty without grace
is the hook without the bait.
Ralph Waldo Emerson

Provisioning

I saw it coming two weeks ago,
the pandemic that's now at our door.
And before it is over we'll see plenty more.
Since the Covid-19 hits more people my age,
I thought to crimp the bug's rampage.
I drew up a list of supplies I need
to enter into isolation for four months, indeed.
This may help a bit to "flatten the curve,"
prevent me from getting sick early
and save a hospital bed.
So, before the run began on supplies,
I had already all that I needed
to, hopefully, get past the coming highs.

If you do not think about your future,
you cannot have one.
John Galsworthy

Figuring

A loose term for assuming, to anticipate, to predict.
That's how I figure the word can be ticked.
Twenty years ago when I presented my course
on Human Evolution and Migration,
it was still held that human evolution
had, because of culture's influence, come to its end.
I scoffed at it, and these days
the fact of continuing human evolution is broadly held.
I thought that Neandertals and Sapiens did not
interbreed.
Well, I did not take into account
that there was some fornication indeed.
There may be quite some life in the galaxy.
But I still figure there's little Intelligence in the Milky
Way.
The Earth being the exception
with the emphasis on "little," I dare say.
Way before the Covid-19 pandemic began
I made preparations to, for four months, go into self-
isolation.

73

Finally, I truly dislike to predict
on this seventeenth day of March 2020
that the economic disruption caused by this bug
will be worse than in Nineteen-o-Eight.
Most folks are still too concerned about infection,
to, as yet, worry about the coming economic correction.

Nothing gives one person so much advantage over another
as to remain always cool and unruffled under all
circumstances.
Thomas Jefferson

Ideology

There are these people, organization,
who hold the principles of evolution
as being false, and in contempt.
They pick and choose what suits their beliefs,
excluding all in their book not spelled,
writings dating from a previous world.
Confined they are and unaware
that their faith is based on fear.

Promise, large promise, is the soul of an advertisement.
Samuel Johnson

Insight

My favorite saying through these past years:
"Shit happens,"
coarse as it is.

Life consists in what a man is thinking of all day.
Ralph Waldo Emerson

How about women?
H.W.

Ignorance 1

Means not knowing, lacking information,
by itself not shameful is.
We all can add to our knowledge.
Yet, when a person does ignore
that which of importance is,
it makes him ignorant for sure
and certainly a dumbass bore.

An honest man nearly always thinks justly.
Jean-Jaques Rousseau

Panic Buying

A most curious thing is happening
when people stock up on what they think they need.
Some store aisles are empty of whatever was there,
but why is it that people load up on toilet paper?
About this oddity I keep wondering a bit.
Such people must be full of ..it.

Pandemic

In twenty-eighteen I was twice near death,
only medical intervention saved my skin.
With ever new ailments popping up,
I was mentally in the dumps,
the worst I had ever been.
Now, my hemolytic anemia and Meniere's disease
are in remission.
I've made my preparations
not to let this darn Covid-19 do me in.
I will help "break the chain," and to "flatten the curve,"
by isolating myself as much as I can.
I had figured what was coming before most folks did,
and laid in supplies for a four months' retreat.
Mind you, I do not expect this pandemic
to be gone in less than four months,
with the worst in the USA,
still ahead in June or July.

For the world and myself
I hope the worst will be over
at the time of my eighty-fourth birthday
on September twenty-nine.
The economic disruption will be the worst
my generation has seen.
And for many of the poor, the unprepared or ignorant
life will be lean.

But what does it mean, the plague?
It's life, that's all.
Albert Camus

Self-discipline

Ah, such ability.
Who can control his feelings
and overcome his weaknesses,
of which he or she must first be aware?
And, gosh, to pursue what one thinks is right
despite the temptation to cast them aside.

A church is a place in which gentlemen
who have never been to heaven
brag about it to persons who will never get there.
Henry Louis Mencken

Maskerade

No, it isn't a masquerade,
a pretense, a false pose, or a facade.
It also is no deception,
but utterly real
when people now wear masks
to protect themselves,
being of the SARS-CoV-2 virus afraid.

He who loves practice without theory
is like the sailor who boards ship without a rudder
and compass and never knows where he may cast.
Leonardo da Vinci

Vanity

My fingers have been slapped
a few times through time,
not for vanity, but for thinking
I knew better of whatever was at stake.
Pride of my country, Germany, also the U.S.
has never been an issue.
I just take it as it is,
with their pros and cons, their achievements,
their failures.
My appearance and accomplishments
I take without pride.
Vanity is excess.
I take things in stride.

If we had no faults we should not take so much pleasure
in noting those of others.
François de La Rochefoucauld

Stages

It's been claimed that Americans,
according to Freudian psych,
are a genital society,
going by their favorite word "fuck."
But the recent panic buying of toilet paper shows
they are still at the anal stage stuck.

Even things that are true can be proved.
Oscar Wilde

Television

With Isolation so much amiss
these days TV a God-send is.
One cannot read all day or,
on a walk, enjoy a breeze.
So, when I turn it on at night,
right then, my RikkiCat walks from my desk
past the TV to the couch alright.
The other eve she stopped before the screen
reared up and clawed it,
something I had never seen.
Did she mistake it for her litter box
trying to whatever cover up, to keep it clean?

What has no shadow has no strength to live.
Czeslaw Milosz

Taste

With their statement
"chaque un à son goût,"
the French voiced a very liberal motto.
(More than an American conservative
could pursue)
"Each to his own taste" the motto states.
But there's a twist one is able to make,
which modifies its original take,
by adding, grammatically incorrect,
the little world "mauvais" to its end.
With this one can succinctly state:
"Each to his own bad taste."

Good humor is the soul's health;
sadness is its poison.
Stanislaw Leszynski

Credo

If anyone is still in doubt
wondering what I'm all about,
go read my fourteen-hundred plus "Poetic Prose."
If that's too much,
you can always opt out.

We build too many walls
and not enough bridges.
Isaac Newton

Cognitive Dissonance

Science requires paradigms to work,
models with an infinite set of information.
Yet paradigms also create expectations
limiting perceptions,
creating "confirmation bias"
and "change blindness."
We selectively notice and remember only
the kind of evidence supporting our expectations.
And we fail to see the anomalies
contradicting expectations.
Antidotes are awareness and skepticism.

I never desired to please the rabble.
What pleased them, I did not learn;
and what I knew was far removed from their understanding.
Epicurus

Respect,

admiration and appreciation I have
for women and men striving for a clear mind,
for their abilities and achievements,
their efforts and resolutions
as far as our biology and upbringing
allow us to leave false knowledge
and superstitions behind.
It, too, extends to the qualities
of our fellow-animals of whatever kind.

Patience is also a form of action.
Auguste Rodin

Preparedness

There is this German saying
"Wie man sich bettet, so liegt man."
"As one beds oneself, one lies."
So apt describing the situation
"Make America Great,"
which it defies.

There are two kinds of failures:
those who thought and never did,
and those who did and never thought.
Laurence Johnston Peter

Deficit of Discipline

What Covid-19 is demonstrating
is the lack of discipline,
the orderly conduct of behavior
across wide swaths of American society.
Not using turn signals, running red lights,
objecting to speed checks, not staying apart,
not staying home.
This pandemic will teach a lesson
by the relative death rate
compared to other countries worldwide.
But hail to the women and men
on the frontline of defense,
the doctors, nurses, checkers,
policemen, and truckers,
who keep civilization going, time and again.

Freedom is not procured by a full enjoyment of what is
desired,
but by controlling the desire.
Epictetus

Reaching Out 1

In these times of physical social distance,
it's interesting to observe
how people deal with this novel situation,
how they communicate, sometimes swerve.
Some email, some call,
some show up for a talk,
of course, six feet apart.
Others keep brooding at home,
many go for a walk.
Cleaning the house or apartment
has become a widespread task.
I wonder what the latter do
when this predicament lasts?
They can always start cleaning again
from where they did start.

Everyone needs help from everyone.
Bertolt Brecht

Views

A centuries-old Juniper tree
blocked a neighbor's view.
He had it cut down
so that obscuring branches
he need no longer look through.
I implored him,
"Look after cutting this beautiful,
age-old tree down,
you must live at least two hundred years
in this house you so briefly own."

Justice is to be found only in the imagination.
Alfred Bernhard Nobel

Reductionism

We have come a long way from Hippocrates and Galen's
medical mumbo jumbo,
the Four Humors,
based largely on superstition and belief,
a paradigm carried forward for two thousand years.
Reductionism reduces complex biological phenomena
into singular parts to better understand their causes.
Medicine's contemporary paradigm
including germ theory.
Specialization has been its result
and better cures have been produced.
But might it be that we have gone too far,
forgotten that bodily functions
are governed by more than a single cause,
that a holistic approach in parallel is called for?
What would a paradigm combining the two look like?
How much more effective might it be?

It is unhealthy to live.
He who lives, dies.
Stanislaw Jerzy Lec

94

Borrowed Time

This pandemic, the Covid-19,
will not be the last our species will see.
Beware and prepare for what's yet to come
I, myself, need not worry,
because I'll be gone.
Let this current pandemic be a warning to all,
for the next may be worse.
We live on borrowed time.

Sometimes people don't want to hear the truth
because they don't want their illusions destroyed.
Friedrich Nietzsche

Commentaries

Plenty of subjects this pandemic provides
to comment about, to wisecrack and chide.
The month of April has just begun,
and the worst, I, nincompoop, predict, is yet to come.
I provisioned myself for a four months run,
well before all the toilet paper was gone.
It will likely peak by June, July,
by August we may again see the sun.
Worldwide, economies will be in dire straits,
more than the experts claim these days.
I feel for the people who've lost their jobs,
and the many small businesses beyond hope.

Much will change.
The USA, I once more predict,
will have the greatest number of infections per capita
and dead
of any big country in the world.
And the question will arise
whether a democratic society like the USA
is truly able to muster the actions
a future pandemic will require.

He that is of the opinion money will do everything
may well be suspected of doing everything for money.
Benjamin Franklin

White Water

I went down the river, twice, the Colorado she is called,
each time in a small inflatable oar-powered boat
some by a couple of women controlled.
I experienced the Grand Canyon from the bottom up,
walking down was not my duck.
Thus we ran the rapids,
held on tight, screamed, and bailed,
and exulted once another rapid had been nailed.
Eleven days each, sleeping under the stars,
exploring side canyons,
swimming in the clean waters of pools
and waterfalls tumbling down from afar.
Once, past the Little Colorado,
the big river was muddy brown,
red she was never, by far.
And, finally, I can proudly claim
I rafted Lava Falls with a woman at the helm.

In the confrontation between the stream and the rock,
the stream always wins – not through strength
but by perseverance.
Buddha

Integrity, Again

There's this narcissistic president of the USA
who waffles, rules by the gut, does not lead,
slavishly followed by the Republican party.
Then, there is Anthony Fauci,
Head of the NIAID,
who speaks truth, speaks his mind,
and demonstrates at a time it is sorely needed,
what integrity means.

Always remember that your decision to be a success
is more important than anything else.
Abraham Lincoln

Bananas

You may recall, I told before,
I've provisioned myself
to have enough food and goodies
to last me in isolation four months or more.
However, all by myself, nuts I might go,
and if that's not enough, bananas too.
But I'll try to make the best of it,
at the end of my driveway open a stand,
where I will sell at a distance of six feet,
whatever's in stock, what I have on hand.
And should I run out of bananas, shucks,
I can always switch over to hawking nuts.

When I'm good, I'm very good.
But when I'm bad, I'm better.
Mae West

Wishful Thinking

There are all kinds of wishful thoughts,
that my eyesight would hold,
that my left knee would not fold.
But what is foremost on my mind,
is to be around two, three more years,
to observe how mankind, hopefully,
will get out of the dumps
and leave the effects of the pandemic behind.
I want to find out if we can overcome
the differences of the past
for a new, a different, a better world,
more just, less rapacious, less dumb.
Thus, before I take my eventual leave
I'd like to find out,
if, of my troublesome species,
I can be proud.

We are what we imagine ourselves to be.
Kurt Vonnegut

Lethargy

A pathological state of sleepiness,
deep-seated unresponsiveness and inactivity.
A lack of energy and enthusiasm.
My condition after two weeks of isolation.

It is in trifles that the mind betrays itself.
Edward George Bulwer-Lytton

Manners

Some are bad, others good.
That they can do without think the ignorant.
When in truth proper manners
serve as social lubricant.

It is absurd to divide people into good or bad.
People are either charming or tedious.
Oscar Wilde

Hemispheres

Not the ones of the earthly domain,
but the left and right of the human brain.
Each controls the body's opposite side.
The left deals with logic,
science, mathematics and such,
with creativity and the arts it is the right.
This is what it says in the charts, simplified.
But then it is claimed that the frontal lobe
controls logical thinking, reasoning,
planning, and organization, also checks emotions
originating in the amygdala, the limbic system.
Well, in my teens I latched onto the idea
that my extended family was too emotional by far.
I wanted to expunge, at least limit this "affliction,"
and strove for more control of undesired emotion.
Through the years my frontal lobes gained more control,
yet every once in a while this control goes AWOL.

Thus, I am quite aware, there's no escape,
that the power of emotion continues to be there.
Nothing's wrong with this when I am touched,
when I deeply feel something, when I deeply care.

Do not walk on the well-trodden path – you may slip.
Sytanislaw Jerzy Lec

Stuff

There is so much to write about
of things which surface in the mind.
Some are mundane, others arcane,
some of wisdom containing a grain.
All require to be put into words
for myself to know,
for others, maybe, also to gain.
Here, I can't help remembring my long-gone friend,
the venerable Michel de Montaigne.

The wise are instructed by reason,
average minds by experience,
the stupid by necessity,
and the brute by instinct.
Marcus Tulles Cicero

Compassion

There's so much crying for compassion,
it's hard to know where to start.
There's far too much suffering in the world,
the misfortunes of people, animals, and plants,
forests and lands,
even Earth itself.
And far too much is caused
by the misdeeds of man himself.

We must always think about things,
and we must think about things as they are,
not as they are said to be.
George Bernard Shaw

Socrates

---

has urged us through the ages,
his words apply not just to sages:
"The unexamined life is not worth living."
There's many a woman and man
who haven't the time
while grubbing for their subsistence.
And many who could, give a damn
to examine their existence.
From this it follows that
the majority of people aren't worth living.
And when worse comes to worst:
I cannot help but wonder
whether a Gaddafi, a Trump,
a Stalin took time for life to ponder.

The secret of man's being is not only to live,
but to have something to live for.
Fyodor Mikhailovich Dostoyevsky

Modus Vivendi

It is said to be an arrangement
between conflicting parties
for an equitable temporary solution,
but also as being
a Way of Life.
If it's both, the latter and former,
is this term indicative
of life at times being equitable,
but also temporary and conflicting?

I am a marvelous housekeeper.
Every time I leave a man
I keep his house.
Zsa Zsa Gabor

Bon Mot

I do love bon mots,
a "good word" here and there.
a witty remark, a quip, a pun.
Some I do produce myself,
but I appreciate them coming from anyone.
I also like using, as per my title up top,
an aphorism, a maxim, a motto,
a saying, an adage, a proverb and such.
But a bon mot tops the entire bunch.

Sometimes you have to be silent to be heard.
Stanislaw Jerzy Lec

Observations

I would like to live a few more years
to observe, to experience,
how our world order will yet rise from Covid-19.
What all will change, for surely much will,
some to the good, some to the ill?
After WWII when things were a mire,
the world came together
by Roosevelt and Marshall inspired.
Who will rise in the years to come
in the West and the East to help overcome
so as not to strife and misery succumb?
A friend of mine, a few days younger,
broadly interested and smart,
three years ago there rang his bell.
Some folks might say he now dwells in hell.
What all he missed that happened since,
but this is what ephemeral life is about,
I too will face the silence still.

If the Republicans stop telling lies about the Democrats,
we will stop telling the truth about them.
Adlai E. Stevenson

111

Past, Present, & Future

To live in the present, ah.
Whoever can?
The past, ever present,
is never quite gone.
Without the past,
how would we steer,
how could we evaluate,
how persevere?
The future, too,
will always creep in.
Without it, how would we ever begin?
Some folks may be able to live in the present,
happily going along.
But most such exceptions, without a tutor,
would have no past and also no future.

People fear silence as they fear solitude,
because both give them a glimpse
of the terror of life's nothingness.
André Maurois

Bite The Bullet

Sooner than later we will have to rise,
in more sense than one,
to the challenge of biting the bullet,
and facing the virus.
Isolation won't protect me/us forever,
and a vaccine is not yet due.
It will not stop until the last human on Earth
has been infected by SARS-CoV-2.
Except for the parochial US news
I haven't heard the word "our planet"
so much in use.
May its use last for years to come
and guide us to a better time.

It is not necessary to understand things
in order to argue about them.
Pierre Auguste Caron de Beaumarchais

113

Slip-sliding Away

Four of my men-friends,
two younger, two older,
in the years that have come and gone,
have taken their leave
without checking with me first
whether it's alright to run.
Five are left, four younger, one older.
Two are sliding,
I, too, don't get bolder.
But my mind still holds up fairly well,
if the body would too
it would truly be swell.

The difference between stupidity and genius
is that genius has its limits.
Albert Einstein

Joy

The other day I made a call
to find a taker for some bird books
published in eighteen-o-ten,
with beautiful illustrations,
in German, of course.
I caught the local Audubon man,
we hit it off, with little talk about birds,
but rather about ourselves,
of God and the world,
for an hour long.
Such a joy it was to find "Intelligence,"
in this seventy-seven year old fellow,
whom I called a kid in my audaciousness.
Covid-19 permitting, we agreed to have lunch
to continue our "God and the world" conversation,
take another plunge.

Tact is the ability to describe others
as they see themselves.
Abraham Lincoln

Happiness vs Contentment

Happy I can be at the spur of a moment
from something or someone
bringing great joy.
But this feeling is fleeting,
as marvelous as it is.
Happy we can't be for infinity.
But contentment, if one is lucky,
can last for a lifetime,
if that is to be.

Life is a tragedy for those who feel
and a comedy for those who think.
Jean de La Bruyere

Asteroid

There orbits at 2.27, 024, 2.2, in the Belt,
an asteroid of about four miles
which carries the name of Herbwindolf.
known at the Minor Planet Center under #20156.
My departed friend Paul Comba,
who discovered it as one of more than one thousand,
announced my namesake at a gathering of friends.
When thanking him I couldn't help saying,
that it was the only way I made it to the heavens.

Every author in some way portrays himself
in his works, even if it be against his will.
Johann Wolfgang von Goethe

Wild Life

Many years ago, when I still was a tyke,
I recall my interest in outdoor life.
In summer I collected little birds
fallen from a nest
and buried them for their final rest.
Much later in life Africa called.
First its history,
later, I became by its wildlife enthralled.
On safaris I saw it in the rough,
these days on TV must be enough.
I abhor violence of any kind,
yet wildlife violence I do not mind.
"Nature, red in tooth and claw,"
is natural, holds me in awe.
Bush walks were my favorite draw,
taking me back to when my ancestors
walked the bush, the savanna.

Violence is the last refuge of the incompetent.
Isaac Asimov

Be Good

These days when I bid good-bye to friends
and other pleasant folk,
I part by saying "Be good."
Not a one has taken it the way I mean,
but rather to be morally understood.
When I then receive a response
that being good is hard to hew to,
it gives me the opportunity to tell them
"Just be good at what you do."

I would never die for my beliefs
because I might be wrong.
Bertrand Russel

119

Fallacy

Covid-19 called for isolation.
I provisioned myself as best I could
with food and medicines for my livelihood,
to last me, if needed, for a period
of up to four months, assured.
I failed to take into account
social separation in isolation, the lack of the vis-à-vis.
Thus I'm relaxing my being alone,
and meet with friends, here and there,
at a goodly distance for some food and a beer.
Sooner or later, the world I must dare,
most likely contract the virus, and see how I'll fare.
It got me to think of future

Mars-bound women and men,
how they will deal with months aplenty
cooped up in the size of a fancy shanty.
How will they tolerate the idiosyncrasies of the crew
without their unity coming askew?
We are social creatures, as far as it goes,
too little isn't enough, too much brings woes.

City life: millions of people being lonesome together.
Henry David Thoreau

Shadows 2

Shadows lie across the Earth.
Illness and hunger waxing apace.
As many as a billion
may die from the SARS-CoV-2 disease,
starvation will bring a few million to their knees.
It isn't that we don't have enough food,
it is the lack of transportation
to get it to where it will do some good.
Will the nations put their quarrels aside
and tackle vaccines together in stride?
The Earth herself will breathe a sigh of relief,
nature will rejoice, the plunder will lessen,
for awhile, at least.

Every sentence that I utter must be understood
not as an affirmation, but as a question.
Niels Bohr

Light 2

Will the Earth turn a bit darker
seen from space at night?
Will stars sparkle brighter once more,
when there is less light?
Might we humans truly shrink
from almost eight billion
down by one?
Might the planet get a reprieve
so that we, as a species, can muddle on?
Might we learn from our present malaise
to strive for a future full of promise?
Might an errant proton from space
knock out a strand of DNA,
for a rare positive mutation,
in time to give rise to a truly sapient species
for a new and better day?

The first human who hurled an insult instead of a stone
was the founder of civilization.
Sigmund Freud

123

Foolhardiness vs Courage

When one hears, reads, and sees
how many people of all walks of life
SARS-CoV-2 took to their graves,
one wonders what they had in common
that their lives found no reprieve.
Thus I keep wondering what to do.
Shall I be foolhardy, step into the world,
or courageously face what I might incur?
In two thousand eighteen I twice faced death,
Now, a year later I have largely overcome
my two worst afflictions, did not succumb.
Should I thus dare, have the courage to try
to expose myself to infection,
either get through it in good steed,
or, maybe, die?

The pure and simple truth is rarely pure
and never simple.
Oscar Wilde

Image 1

It is said that man was created
in the image of God.
Well, man defecates as every animal does.
And what are the manners of this imagined God
based on all that man does cause.

When you want to fool the world,
tell the truth.
Otto von Bismarck

125

Water

Too much in Florida,
not enough in the Southwest.
Yet they keep building.
What is it they miss?
There are the fools cluttering up the coasts,
building and selling for money, of course.
Then come the buyers who think far ahead,
ha, at most a few years,
not that rising waters will catch them dead.
Eventually they will need to helicopter
to their pads.
And water will dwindle ever more
for the folks dwelling and moving southwest.
Are the builders ignorant on this score?
But money, money is all they want.
They don't give a damn
for what they do to the land.

Indeed, history is nothing more than a tableau
of crimes and misfortunes.
Voltaire

Insects

Did I observe correctly last year,
and the current one, two-thousand-twenty, too,
that fewer insects have made their debut?
In one respect this is nothing to complain,
bugs can be a bane, if not a pain.
And is my other observation right
that there are fewer birds, alright?
Is our ecosystem going down the drain?
We do need the birds and the bees
not just for kids to explain
where they came from
and lo, where they are going to,
once insects and birds become deja-vu.

Confidence is what you have
before you understand the problem.
Woody Allen

Propagation

One more year it is that I get to hear
the hooting of owls at the break of dawn.
Later the plaintive call of mourning doves.
Males claiming their territory,
calling for females in their labor of love,
chasing them hither and yon,
for a new generation to be born..
Nice it would be to hear them again next year.
It's okay if it's so,
but I also give a hoot if it's not to be.

Common sense is the collection of prejudices
acquired by age eighteen.
Albert Einstein

Priorities

Ah, the choices I need to make!
And at eighty-three which of three
medical cases to undertake?
The left knee needs surgery, two molars need a crown.
But neither is needed if I terminate isolation
and won't survive the SARS-CoV-2 countdown.
Last night I decided,
on this twenty-ninth of April 2020,
it's no use fiddling around.
I must face reality to be on solid ground.
I shall live life as I normally do.
The virus may eventually get me.
Then I'll see how I'll do.
Should I make it, then I know where I stand.
If I don't, it's okay. There's always this other land.
The only question I have left,
is who will take care of my RikkiCat?

When the heroes go off the stage,
the clowns come on,
Heinrich Heine

129

Infinity

I sit on a boulder in my yard,
Rikki behind me exploring her world.
Conscious awareness is mine while it lasts.
The wind sings to me in the bushes and trees,
a bouquet of yellow flowers grows next to my feet.
All this must end, no more sensations,
no longer being of this world, no more observations.
Yet I can't help imagining what all I have been,
what my molecules, my elements have already seen.
Did some trod the Earth in a triceratops,
and before grace a carboniferous fern?
What will yet happen to my few remains?
The biome of my very Self
will, too, go the way of all earthly things,
expire in the flames the fire will bring.

But then,
somewhere away from the rush of the world,
my ashes will be dispersed by the wind,
rain will wash some into the earth.
Will my molecules, my atoms, my elements,
nourish yet other beings in life's marvelous sea,
a nematode in the soil, a leaf on a tree?
Will a browsing doe's milk feed her fawn yet to be?
Might I grace the world in a flower's bloom?
Lucky me if a tree's roots take me in
and in a juniper I live for a few hundred years.
I shall be recycled, it's nature's design,
in the Earth, in Life, engulfed by the sun.
I am infinite.
Infinity is mine.

At the touch of love everyone becomes a poet.
Plato

Being Fast

I've often claimed that I am fast,
it being my strength and failure.
On the whole it has served me fairly well.
I am who I am. It is my nature.

A man cannot be comfortable
without his own approval.
Mark Twain

Composing

I do not brood over what I've written.
At times I fiddle with it. Mostly I don't.
As it spills from my mind, I put it in writing.
At times I compose a verse
sitting on a rock in the yard,
or an idea gestates while driving my car.
Some nights I still hit on an idea
and need to get up for I can't fall asleep
since by daylight the idea is no longer there.
The process is ad hoc at best.
Sometimes a verse turns out a bit better.
At other times I am not so blessed.

Do not be too timid and squeamish about your actions.
All life is an experiment.
Ralph Waldo Emerson

Peripatetic Teacher

In the dining room on the sideboard stands
a carving of Nafesi Mpagua, of Makonde tribal lands.
In eighty-nine we safaried in Tanzania.
Upon its conclusion in Arusha,
we entered a souvenir store with Niko, our guide.
Among the touristy carvings
my wife spotted a unique figurine.
A peripatetic teacher, books on his head,
carrying a calabash and backpack,
a pupil by his legs, both with staffs in hand.
By its very self the figure took command!
Too heavy to carry home it was to be shipped.
When it did not come, Niko got the shipment done.
For thirty years it stood, right next to where we eat.
In all this time not a diner paid attention to it,
inquired, showed interest, found it neat.
Not a single guest! Ignorance be excused.
To have it, we are blessed.

There is no such thing on earth as an uninteresting subject;
the only thing that can exist is an uninterested person.
Gilbert Keith Chesterton

Moderation

To do things moderately,
but regularly, too,
is what I grew up with in Germany.
What a surprise it was
when I came to the U.S.
The motto here was:
Do everything in excess.

Everything in excess is opposed to nature.
Hippocrates

Discipline

Not the soldier-kind,
but rather the one controlled by the mind.
The assertion of willpower over basic desire,
self-control, the initiative to get started,
to overcome hardships,
the will to persevere, not to expire.

No man is free who is not master of himself.
Epictetus

The Saltwater Crocodile

In the year eighty-five
I traveled Australia's east coast by myself.
In Townsville, at the end of my trip,
I walked into a souvenir store on a blip.
An aboriginal woman appeared from the back.
I had just acquired my anthro degree.
In no time the two of us were deeply into anthropology.
We had the time; no other clients came in to see.
I selected a typical aboriginal work of art
of the saltwater crocodile, Numanwari,
by the artist Bubawanga, son of Mannalwanga.
The croc being too large, it was shipped.
Most precious were the kudos
the aboriginal lady extended to me
for me having chosen a true native painting.

You can give without loving,
but you can never love without giving.
Robert Louis Stevenson

139

Duty

It is not the legal obligation here at stake,
the superficial, rule-based exhortation,
but rather its underlying moral responsibility,
the root of decency.

What religion a man shall have is a historical accident,
quite as much as what language he shall speak.
George Santayana

Image 2

We all evolve an image of the world,
how it ought or ought not to be.
Society puts its stamp on it,
but being part of it,
also the individual's family.
Some people grow up in the shadows of night,
others experience the brightness of light.
Benighted folks act out the darkness they live in.
Enlightened people rejoice in the beauty they bring.

Opinions alter, manners change, creeds rise and fall,
but the moral laws are written on the table of eternity.
John Acton

Shona

Ah, Victory Falls. Mosi-oa-Tunya.
The Smoke-that-Thunders.
Known for centuries to natives by this name
before Livingston made it known to the world
and named it after his queen.
We ventured there in ninety-seven
experienced the Falls from the Zimbabwean side.
A helicopter ride was the best of the sight.
Three times a day we ventured back and forth
to watch Zambezi's waters rush into the gorge.
We walked from store to local store,
found serpentine Shona sculptures and more.
The one we chose, its artist unknown.
The human figure, contemplative,
its name certain to last, so appropriate these days:
"Thinking about the Past."

In a time of drastic change,
it is the learners who inherit the future.
The learned usually find themselves equipped
to live in a world that no longer exists.
Eric Hoffer

Quest

Every human worth his salt
sets out on a life-long quest.
Most do it early, some do it later,
some more superficial, others deeper.
What counts is that it's done at all.
At issue is the meaning of life,
with each of the searchers, lucky to be,
to arrive at his own story, the apogee,
whose insights he can then apply to life,
for better or worse,
for success or for strife.

Drinking when we are not thirsty
and making love all year round, madam,
that is all there is to distinguish us from other animals.
Pierre Auguste Caron de Beaumarchais

Note "other."
H.W.

144

Charisma

What is it that gives some people
a compelling attractiveness, a presence, an appeal?
For a woman I would add charm and allure,
but also intelligence and character, for sure.
These characteristics come in doses small and great.
Some can be evil, like in a Hitler.
Humane, subdued and humble, they are
as shown by Nelson Mandela.

There is no greatness where there is not simplicity.
Lev Nikolaevich Tolstoy

Tempora Mutantur

---

et nos mutamur in illis.
"Times change and we change with them."
So known already in Roman times.
Imagine a woman born in nineteen-hundred-ten
in what was the German emperor state then.
In her teens she lived through a decade
of democracy.
In her twenties she experienced Hitler's tyranny.
Had she lived in the east of the Reich,
she would have seen the communist tyranny ending
at seventy-nine.
Lucky for her, then came democracy.
Five times, times changed, and she with them
through stories on how to live,
concocted by changed men.

The less we know the more we suspect.
Henry Wheeler Shaw

Alone

Alone we once thought to be on Earth
amongst the beasts of air, land, and sea.
Sun, planets, and the stars revolved around us.
We were the center of our universe. –
Only a hundred years have passed
since we've learned of the cosmos so vast.
And now we are searching the heavens far and wide
to find whether there's other life out there,
similar to our kind.
Might it turn out that there is life,
scum in some seas, a metazoan?
Or will it be shown that we are truly alone?

Can we rework the calendar
so that we don't have to live in the twentieth century?
Stanislaw Jerzy Lec

Reaching Out 2

Is wondering what our fellow men and women are
about?
To care, to explore, to trust and to doubt;
not just for people but all the world we live in.
To learn, to comprehend, to understand.
Not staying confined with their heads stuck in sand.

I quote others only in order to better
to express myself.
Michel de Montaigne

148

One of a Kind

The way we and nature developed our mind,
we can say we are one of a kind,
but more so even of one kind.
There are no races, only ethnic groups.
Yet prejudices against each other
keep our minds confined.

It is in self-limitation that the master shows himself.
Johann Wolfgang von Goethe

Taken For Granted

Covid-19 has shown that all we've taken for granted
isn't assured, but virus-prone.
Most important for some folks
is getting plenty of toilet paper rolls.
Food items become scarce, prices go up.
Shops are closed, restaurants are on pick-up.
Doctors communicate by Internet,
hair grows ever longer with barbers beset
since a distance of six feet cannot be met.
The same holds true when friends we meet,
we can no longer hug, a social treat,
provided isolation lets us get out from our retreat.
Vacations and flights are out of sight.
Oh, and masks should be worn
to stay safe from the virus's blight.
Globalization is going to suffer.
What all will yet change?
Will it be the dawning of a new age?

If you cannot do what you wish,
you should wish what you can do.
Terence

Manus Manum Lavat

"One hand washes the other,"
known already in Roman times
and ages before for sure.
Yet some people have no idea
that it's also called reciprocity.
They easily take what's been given to them,
then sit on their derrières.

You cannot teach a man anything;
you can only help him discover it in himself.
Galileo Galilei

151

Pecularities

Getting south of the equator
the sky appears skewed.
The first time I saw it,
it certainly looked weird.
The constellations are upside down
and the sun rises to the right.
All due to the 23.5 degrees
of the Earth's tilt.

Information is not knowledge.
Albert Einstein

Tattoos

The Marquesas would have been my final trip
had Menière's disease not put a stop to it.
These islanders invented the tattoo.
Contemporary fads,
tattoos, rings in ears, also lips, noses and mouths,
I, however, most dearly eschew.
On a man I find tattoos oft looking déjá vu.
On women they become a stain.
I rather like my women plain.

The vast majority of human beings dislike and even dread
all notions with which they are not familiar.
Hence, it comes about that at their first appearance
innovators have always been derided as fools and madmen.
Aldous Huxley

Spider

On my window sill,
glistening in the morning sun,
glories a delicate, dense spider net
a busy spider has spun.
The first time I noticed it,
I took it down.
When, next morning,
at breakfast, it was back,
ever more beautiful.
I didn't have the heart
to destroy the diligent spider's
work again.
So, now, at breakfast,
in the morning sun,
I marvel at what this tiny spider has spun.

The way to love anything is to realize
that it might be lost.
Gilbert Keith Chesterton

Paradise

There was this couple in paradise,
who lived innocently like animals, never knew vice.
Then it so happened they ate
from the tree of knowledge,
took the snake's bait.
Ever since tempting females and snakes
had to be put in their proper place.
Now that the proverbial couple knew
the difference between good and evil,
they were expelled from the Garden of Eden.
Gone was the innocence, now they could reason.
Science calls it, through millions of years acquired
– consciousness –
evolved from an ape-size brain,
to today's Homo sapiens domain.
Ever since humans have fought
wrongness and evil when we aught
to promote wellbeing and goodness,
but so often for naught.

155

Yet there is hope, for we do know today
that in olden times we acted worse.
Consciousness has also helped us
to fight the choice of this terrible curse.

The face of the enemy frightens me only
when I see how much it resembles mine.
Stanislaw Jerzy Lec

Worthless

What is the worth of a woman or man
if they no longer can
contribute to the society they belong?
When they become a strain to maintain,
draw on ever scarcer resources to sustain.
When they rarely through their productive life
contributed an equivalent to now keep them alive.
When they burden generations to come
with expenses, until they succumb.
The credo of the sanctity of life
will eventually wreck societies.
Its question is rife.

He who has lived a day has lived an age.
Jean de La Bruyere

Death is not the worst that can happen to man.
Plato

He who knows that enough is enough will always have
enough.
Lao Tzu

Husbandry

----

is known as the care and cultivation
of animals and crops.
Grooming means to clean and brush.
A groom is a wedding man.
I've always wondered how husbandry
might relate to husband.
And why the groom?
Am I mistaken? Is it an illusion?
Why does the groom becoming husband –
require cleaning, brushing, care and cultivation?
How come only male terms
are connected with husbandry and grooming?
Seemingly female humans have no need
for such allusions.

Those who can think, but cannot express what they think,
place themselves at the level of those who cannot think.
Pericles

Concoctions 2

----

also known as fabrications.
Unbelievable what people are able to believe.
From todays lies, conspiracies, and misrepresentations
to the age-old wish for life after death,
the fear of loss of consciousness,
and if not heaven, at least rebirth.
From simple distortions of veracity,
to the truths all major religions have claimed,
man has concocted, fabricated stories,
the most elaborate ancient Egyptians framed.
Not to forget for what Catholics, Muslims, Hindus,
Mayas, Aztecs, Shintos, and others,
ad infinitum, have aimed.
Adherents of Buddhism and Confucianism
kept themselves to ethics restraint.
And is science, the pursuit of disprovable truths,
not just another belief?

However many holy words you read, however many you
speak,
what good will they do you if you do not act upon them?
Buddha

How To

To be loved is precious,
to be wanted, too.
To be accepted is desirable.
To be tolerated is tolerable.
To be rejected depends on a point of view.

If you don't love me, it does not matter,
anyway, I can love for both of us.
Stendhal

Ignorance 2

Through the years I've read
much science and watched
science shows on TV.
I learned and absorbed plenty
but it occurred to me
how little I truly know,
what I lack to call myself a cognoscenti.
I know a little of this and that,
on some subjects a bit more.
On others I fall flat.
Come to think of it,
one cannot know all.
I never wanted to be a specialist,
didn't have the patience for one.
I rather wanted to be a generalist
as far back as I can recall.

The accent of a man's native country
remains in his mind and his heart,
as it does in his speech.
François de La Rochefoucauld

Morning Sun

After breakfast,
my ablutions done,
I enjoy sitting on my couch
facing the warmth of the morning sun.
Closing my eyes,
an hour later I wake up again.

All life is an experiment.
The more experiments you make the better.
Ralph Waldo Emerson

Prednisone

Two plus years ago, for my hemolytic anemia,
I was prescribed 80 mg of prednisone a day.
By now I'm down to five.
When I was taking only ten a year ago
I asked my hematologist what would happen
should I decide the medication to forego.
"Three days later," he said, "you'd be dead."
I wonder whether the 5 mg I'm now taking
would have the same effect?

As long as people believe in absurdities,
they will commit atrocities.
Voltaire

Kindred Spirit

Rarely does one find,
as one saunters through life,
a woman or man
– oh, what a joy it is –
who dare bare their mind,
to stand naked before you,
yet never lose the dignity of their
spirit, their soul.
Kindred they are,
one of a kind.

Don't walk behind me; I may not lead.
Don't walk in front of me; I may not follow.
Just walk beside me and be my friend.
Albert Camus

Curriculum Vitae

1936, born in Wiesbaden, Germany
1942, age 5, I recall my first memories
       and we vacationed in Bavaria
1943, age 6, once more we spent time in Bavaria
1944, age 7, the bombing started and
       literally scared the shit out of me,
       and I was taken to friends in the country
1945, age 8, the war came to an end
1946, age 9, schooling again began
1947, age 10, to the Gymnasium I was sent,
       with English on the curriculum
1949, age 13, I had to do the Quarta again
1950, age 14, I wasn't material to learn
       shucked from the Gymnasium to a
       blue-color apprenticeship
1953, age 16, I passed with flying colors,
       and good at technical drawing was
       offered a job in this metier
1956, age 19, itching to see the world,
       I motorcycled through Libya, and Egypt

1957, age 20, the world opened up, and among
        other exploits, a girlfriend snapped me up

1960, age 23, work stint in Paris

1961, age 24, married Ute, love of my life,
        age 25, son Dirk born

1962, age 26, daughter Kirsten born

1963, age 27, daughter Karen born

1964, age 27, three children in tow, itching to
        still see more of the world, Canada called

1970, age 33, sales mgr. in Chicago I became

1972, age 35, falling up the ladder: mng. director,
        building up the decrepit company again
        Starting worldwide travels

1977, age 41, put my marriage on the line

1982, age 45, engaging my German successor,
        fatally ill returning to Germany in 1989

1990, age 53, scrambling to keep company going

1991, age 55, highest sales. Ending employment
        Consulting, renewed part-time employment until
        2001. Move to Prescott, AZ
        Begin book translations, writing poetry

Summer 1960 age 23 in Paris

1994, age 58, facilitated courses at adult education
        center
2001, age 64, begin self-importing from Germany
2008, age 72, final retirement
2015, age 78, Ute moving out
2018, age 81, survived twice through medical
        intervention, pacemaker, hemolytic anemia &
        Menière's
2020, age 83, remission of both afflictions,
        lived in Prescott 27 years,
        married to Ute 59, know each other 69 years,
        still alive.

Alas, after a certain age every man is responsible for his face.
Albert Camus

September 2019 age 83   Photo by Elke

Waffle

There's breakfast,
a pecan waffle topped with maple syrup,
maybe even fruit and whipped cream.
Then, there's the waffle
of people failing to make up their mind.
The former is sweet,
the latter a boring kind.

A timid person is frightened before a danger,
a coward during the time, and a courageous person
afterwards.
Jean Paul Richter

Opening Up

Why is it so hard for men to forego
the protection of their male ego?
Might there be none whatsoever, zero?
Might they lack access
to their more emotional side?
Or, is there none,
that there's nothing to hide?
Might they reveal too much of themselves,
afraid to lose their manliness in the process?

Our misdeeds are easily forgotten
when they are known only to ourselves.
François de La Rochefoucauld

Locked Up

Reading this term, what first comes to mind,
is being locked up in a prison of some kind.
But our brains are imprisoned in the skull,
rarely able to truly join the world,
our fellow beings, or not at all.
Why are so many afraid to open the prison?
Need they protect their successes and faults?
Are they afraid to be misunderstood,
to be rejected for being no good?
Oh, what enrichment it is to be
with the gate open,
the mind free.

The worst solitude is to be destitute
of sincere friendship.
Francis Bacon

Entrapped

Many are entrapped by the mindset they hold,
failing to realize what the wider world is about,
the variant of thought that makes it go round.
Some such ideas we'd better forget,
but the majority are no threat.
Some mindsets turn destructive and evil,
ending in such people's fatal upheaval.
Many are happily carried by their mindsets along.
But I can't help but wonder
to what extend, I, in this matter belong?

The greater intellect one has, the more originality
one finds in men.
Ordinary persons find no difference between men.
Blaise Pascal

Teutonic

During the Völkerwanderung
tribes moved all across Europe.
Two thousand years ago,
the Teutons and Cimbri traveled south,
causing the Romans alarm,
doing some legions "a bit of harm."
At last the Romans put a stop to the plunder.
Before the final battle, to save them from slavery,
the Teutons killed their women and children,
then faced their slaughter by the Roman army.
Today, in the Anglo-Saxon world,
Teutonic is synonymous with being German.
Did they have honor, these barbaric Teutons?
Did they have respect, esteem, integrity,
uprightness, honesty, and more?

Or were they just stubborn, choosing death over life?
But what would life have been under Roman rule,
the end of their valour?

I would rather be exposed to the inconveniences
attending too much liberty
than those attending too small a degree of it.
Thomas Jefferson

Sayings

----

of which many there are.
One of which everyone knows is:
"Great minds think alike."
Yet I haven't found a single one
who knows how this saying continues, is going on.
Maybe the below contrivance from my very own quiver
added some profound insight to American parlance.
"Fools never differ."

Most fools think they are only ignorant.
Benjamin Franklin

Anger

What is the root of anger?
Injury, frustration, ego, or fear?
How is it acquired?
How is it controlled,
when one knows, has been taught,
that it isn't one's better nature.
Equanimity should be one's goal?
When anger turns into fury,
blind rage takes over one's soul,
for insanity to take control.

Anger, if not restraint, is frequently more hurtful to us
than the injury that provokes it.
Lucius Annaeus Seneca

Hatred

While I've known anger,
hatred is foreign to me.
Strong dislike or resentment
I may have felt at times in the past.
But one can only hate something
that is stronger than oneself,
I agree.
But then, true evil never crossed my path,
maybe?

All violence, all that is dreary and repels,
is not power, but the absence of power.
Ralph Waldo Emerson

Deep Purple

There, the other day, before me
grew a beautiful deep purple leaf,
Cotinus grace smoke tree.
I looked it up to make sure that's what it was.
In a flight of imagination
my mind traveled far into space,
to a planet of a K-type, red dwarf star,
its close orbit making days a year.
Tide-locked, the proximal hemisphere
is in eternal light.
The far side in the cold of perpetual night.
The star's longer red wavelength radiation,
would tint the planet's vegetation.
What would a deep purple world look like
against our G-type, yellow sun's green,
if life, unlikely, could have evolved there,
could ever have been?

If the facts don't fit the theory,
change the facts.
Albert Einstein

Antagonism,

----

is as opposition or active hostility defined.
It exists between two groups of people.
No respect is extended to either side.
Its lack all too often justified.
Confrontation is more fatal to the weaker
whenever it does not by the rules of the stronger abide.
Cultural differences are at the core of the divide.
When the two sides collide,
their antagonism is reinforced,
perpetuated in the mind.
Examples persist, dear reader, in past and present,
for you to find.

Anger will never disappear so long as thoughts of resentment
are cherished in the mind. Anger will disappear just as soon
as
thoughts of resentment are forgotten.
Buddha

Rationality

A commodity in short supply.
Beware. Intelligence and education are no protection
from irrationality,
as shown by anti-vaccination and conspiracies.
Foremost it means not being beholden
by engrained beliefs,
idiosyncratic ones or society's.
To be skeptical, go by the facts,
think contrarian, not by what attracts.
Justify beliefs, have sensible goals.
Act in accord with moral principles.
Be consistent. Inconsistency is irrational.
And be altruistic for the well-being
of your spirit, your soul.

I believe I have found the missing link
between animals and civilized man.
It is us.
Konrad Lorenz

181

Proud

When I see an atrocity committed,
I feel sad belonging to humankind.
When, of a good deed I hear about,
belonging to this species
makes me joyful, even proud.

If you have knowledge
let others light their candles with it.
Winston Churchill

182

Altruism

Wolves seem to be doing it, birds too.
To raise the next generation, older siblings stay on
when they could leave for a life of their own.
By staying they gain security and learning.
When the time comes, they leave without returning.
Altruism in humans seems to be a selfless concern,
irregardless of gender, ethnicity, class, young and old.
So why do we do something
that looks like fool's gold?
Well, in some deep recesses of our mind
it makes us feel good, a better kind.

Self-discipline is that which, next to virtue,
truly and essentially raises one man above another.
Joseph Addison

183

Prejudice

I hold no preconceived opinions
on gender or ethnic difference
that are not based on reason
or actual experience.
An anthropologist at heart, study, and mind,
I hold no prejudices of any kind.
Yet, I am acutely aware
when I interact with people different than me,
be that sex, ethnicity, color, or nationality.
And if there are few things I am proud to say,
it is that my children appear not to harbor
any prejudices, as far as I can see.

No one ever became thoroughly bad
all at once.
Decimus Junius Juvenal

Charles Darwin

If I had heroes Charles Darwin would be one,
who liberated mankind from long-held
dogmatic beliefs, dearly held,
but patently wrong.
He had the courage to speak up and pronounce
that we are evolved from lower animals,
that Lyell's Earth is old,
much older than the Bible claims,
and man is not a creation of God.
Had I to add another admired man,
it would be a soulmate of mine.
Richard Feynman.

Questions show the mind's range,
and answers its subtlety.
Joseph Joubert

Encounters

I swam the waters of Lake Toba,
sailed the lagoon of Bora Bora.
This I wrote in "Beauty" years past,
but plenty more places I passed, everlast.
The age old mansions in Alamos.
Eating choucroute garni in Alsace.
The giant sand dune I climbed
at the edge of the Sahara in early morn
to watch the rise of the sun.
Walks along the Napali Coast.
The Granada Alhambra and Cordoba Mosque.
The train ride up Copper Canyon.
Camping in the Campi Flegrei, an Italian volcano.
Whale watching in Baja and kayaking its lagoons.
Spotting whales in Icelandic bays
from high in the swinging crow's nest,
when down below, fellow travelers to Neptune sacrificed.
Running the rapids of the Colorado and Snake.

Climbing San Francisco's Humphry's Peak.
Canoeing the Boundary Waters and Quetico.
Walking the Istanbul bazaar.
Seeing the arches and hoodoos in Utah and Arizona.
The cruise through the Society Isles.
Watching a zebra taken by lions.
Being chased by elephants in Botswana.
Admiring Iguazu and Victoria Falls.
Catamaran sailing through the Whitsunday isles.
Snorkeling the Moorea Lagoon.
Walking the town of Rothenburg.
Marvelling at Antelope Canyon.
Driving along the delights of Highway One.
Passing the glaciers in the Drake Passage.
Climbing the tower of Notre Dame.
Seeing the glory of Barrier Reef.
There were St. Kitts, Trinidad, and Tobago.
The pleasure of the shore of Tamariu.
Hikes in Tuscany, Umbria, Burgundy and Provence.
Venturing through Rome and Florence.

Barm- and Grubsee memory jaunt.
Driving Glacier Highway in our Vanagon.
The haunting echos rising from Copper Canyon.
Crossing the coastal Redwood cathedrals.
Wading Pacific temperate rain forests.
Discovering the beauty of Vänern Lake.
The balloon ride over Masai Mara.
The drive across Ngorongoro crater.
First look into Grand Canyon.
The multidinous bleatings on the Serengeti.
The intense human connection with an RN
on a two hour flight from Iguazu to Buenos Aires,
and with a linguist flying from Livingstone to Joburg.
Seeing the pictures in the Altamira caves.

The cure for boredom is curiosity.
There is no cure for curiosity.
Dorothy Parker

Impoverished Nachos

I introduced some friends of mine,
to nachos, believe it or not.
They keep raving about them,
wanted to make them themselves,
and kept asking for the ingredients,
the process, and where I bought what.
I kept saying there's nothing to it:
plenty of corn tortilla chips, black beans,
shredded sharp cheddar, jalapeño slices,
medium salsa, and sour cream.
Put the first three under the broiler
but don't brown the cheese to an extreme.
When this is done, eat this calorie bomb,
if need be, with a team.
The other day, another friend,
sent me a picture of her "nachos-pretend."
They didn't look anything like my beloved muchachos,
which is why I called them impoverished nachos.

Tact in audacity consists in knowing
how far we may go too far.
Jean Cocteau

Gin 'n Tonic

My psycho-friend, upon his descent
from up where he lives, down to my place,
likes to imbibe in my company,
here and there, in a gin 'n tonic,
to a toast we raise to,
well, you know, who's deserved demise.

Patriotism is the last refuge of the scoundrel.
Samuel Johnson

Doormats

There once was the Pied Piper of Hamelin,
who, playing his tempting flute, lured,
then rid that town of its rats.
Would only the pied piper of the USA depart
taking along his beloved doormats.

One should forgive ones enemies,
but not before they are hanged.
Heinrich Heine

Isolation

We are now into our fourth month of isolation,
at least those who are taking it seriously enough.
This, in the Year of the Lord two-thousand-twenty,
today, instead of AD called CE.
Most of my friends are of that age
when getting the virus could mean departure
from life's stage.
One of them, who doesn't want to be named,
adamantly wants isolation to maintain.
Most of these Dears still don't want to be caught
having lunch with me at a restaurant.
There is, however, the odd, dear soul who does and did,
hug me, with both of us wearing our masks, like ghouls.
Another couple, cagey at first,
is now relenting, wanting to "get their life back,"
don't want any longer to be penned up in their shack.
Most of us, the entire population,
feel deprived of what they see as being their lives.
I, myself, still maintain a so-so isolation,
wear a mask when I am among people,

hoping for an eventual vaccine
and being spared by the pandemic, Covid-19.
Not paranoid, I go to town for some provisions.
I may have acquired a cavalier attitude
escaping death twice in two-thousand-eighteen.
Mornings and also prior to dusk
I sit with Rikki, my cat,
on a boulder in my yard or on my deck.
We contemplate whatever there is of minor events.
What else is there to do with the slowdown of the world?
We enjoy the silence the virus has brought,
one positive versus its misery, its terrible onslaught.
And the latest now, while I continue to write,
is that infections in the U.S. are on the rise.
At the end of March I predicted already
that the worst would yet in June & July arise.
Many people are too cavalier,
paying for their want to live life,
but they also need to make a living,
get ahead, make efforts to strive.
My psycho-friend, up on the hill,
enjoys a visit with me every other day.

We sit apart wherever we please,
enjoy a drink and chew the fat,
with me restraining him not to tear,
guess who, psychoanalized, to piece after piece.
And now, with the riots and demonstrations galore,
distancing neglected ever more,
the virus will be happy for more victims to score.
All this will end with the USA
having the most per capita deaths
with the world to share.

Man perfected by society is the best of all animals;
he is the most terrible of all
when he lives without law and without justice.
Aristotle

Accustomed

"I've grown accustomed to her face,"
so goes the song of Fair Lady.
Thus, through the decades I have too
become endeared with your little gestures,
your voice, your telling of stories,
your pursuit of spirituality, your love of nature,
your cooking, your interruptions, your smile,
your need for independence, your scent, your very you.
The many things we shared,
the many things we have in common,
the likeness of our physiques,
and, all in all, how well we have fared.
Fifty-nine years it will be this year,
we have shared through joys and strife.
And, with some luck, we may discover
seventy years of knowing each other.
All the above being, oh, so true,
I cannot help but loving you.

All glory comes from daring to begin.
William Shakespeare

Blind Sighted

Note the spelling in two words.
I am neither using blindsighted
in place of the correct blindsided term
nor in its meaning of blindsided.
Rather it conveys that someone's sight is blind
from being able to see what ought to be seen.
Worse it becomes when two sides
hold engrained views expressed in specific ways,
which perpetuate what ails their relationship.
The curse of slavery is haunting the USA.
The riots these days follow the killing
of George Floyd and other Blacks.
The militarized police of this country
all too often have reasons to think in terms of race,
just as Blacks from long experience
have justified reasons for being singled out
for often minor offenses by police.

When the two parties become engaged,
the Blacks, instead of playing possum,
react all too often with justified anger,
causing a corresponding reaction by the police.
The American police force,
often insufficiently trained, is too frequently allowed
drastic application of force,
coming from an, at base, violent society,
and is prone to apply force with devastating results.
The ready use of firearms is seemingly a holdover
from the Wild West.
Both sides re-in-force their behavior.
Neither side is able to see beyond
of it's being blind sighted.

Words are loaded pistols.
Jean Paul Sartre

Encounter

Once more, in the morning,
sitting in my yard on one
of the boulders in the early sun,
out of the bushes trundles a javelina,
who, with his poor eyesight, keeps coming on.
Then he stops and we face each other
until he catches my scent.
Sitting still, I'm certain what he will do next.
To retreat from this human, he must think, is best.

Believe those who are seeking the truth.
Doubt those who find it.
Andre Gide

Chocolate Chip Cookies

Many times, as I've said before,
for chocolate chip cookies,
it was worth coming to America.
But had I known what has become of it,
I wonder, I wonder,
was it right what I did?

The art of pleasing is the art of deception.
Luc de Clapiers de Vauvenargues

Alcohol

The Arabs gave us al-kuhl, this pleasant term,
just as sugar, al-sukar, they did.
Otherwise known as ethanol or spirit.
Throughout my life I've liked to tipple a bit
but never became dependent on it.
Now, that eighty-three years of age I've hit,
the aftereffects of a single drink
tell me the time has come to eventually quit.

Self-discipline is that which, next to virtue,
truly and essentially raises one man above another.
Joseph Addison

Foible

I have a foible for women.
It must come from the female part in me.
Happily, I also relate with men,
but have no desire a he-man to be.
Never did I impose myself on women,
but rather let things fall into place.
So, if a foible is called a weakness,
my weakness for women is not a disgrace.

If the art of conversation stood a little higher
we would have a lower birthrate.
Stanislaw Jerzy Lec

Contradictions

Both Bible and Qu-ran
contain a goodly number of contradictions.
Their adherents claim there are none.
This tells what faith can accomplish
for believers to keep holding on.

A sane person to an insane society
must appear insane.
Kurt Vonnegut

Departures

Some are quick,
some drag on for years.
Quick are the heart attacks, a stroke,
a hiatal hernia, or cancer, severe.
Then there are the cases
where body or mind fade,
fall slowly apart.
The question is?
Which is the better way to depart?

The young man who has not wept is a savage
and the old man who will not laugh is a fool.
George Santayana

Hair

A woman's pride.
Natural is what I like.
Too bad, conservative Muslims require it to hide.
Yet their beards proclaim manhood,
as they claim for their side.
In the West, scientists are the wearers of beards.
What is it that they have to guard?
These days scruffy beards are all the rage.
How did this fashion enter the stage?
Bald pates, like billiard balls, are sexy, too,
but those aren't really something new.
And what I've heard, who knows if it's true,
some folks shave their entire statue.
Twice I grew a short-time beard
when conditions in this direction turned.
Yet it was but a circumstantial fad,
for I felt I looked like Yasser Arafat.

Everything has been said before, but since nobody listens
we have to keep going back and begin all over again.
Andre Gide

Sociability

Some people are sociable,
others are not.
I wonder what induces the "some,"
to engage with their fellow beings,
be friendly, amicable, cordial,
hospitable, on the spot,
are open to new experience,
find out what the world is about?
There are some
who must be pulled from their lair,
to then turn out to be quite fair.
But the "others" are withdrawn,
a hopeless lot.
Why do they stay isolated
instead of engaging the world?
Are they enough to themselves
with solitude preferred?

There would be no society if living together
depended upon understanding each other.
Eric Hoffer

205

Reinforcement

It's not impossible, but maybe,
I discovered how people maintain their ideology.
They mouth it at every opportunity.

A little sincerity is a dangerous thing,
and a great deal of it is absolutely fatal.
Oscar Wilde

206

Structure

----

in life, a coherent pattern of organization,
is a measure of success.
To procure structure requires discipline
resulting in order.
A deficit of order causes chaos.
A surfeit of structure results in stasis
and eventual ruin.
Balance, thus, is the conclusion.

Method is the arithmetic of success.
Henry Weiler Shaw

The Curse

Why the "post-paradise" cruelty
and wanton destruction?
Because it is easier to destroy than to build.
Unregulated consciousness ruled.
Stories were devised to channel this drive.
And God blessed them and said to them,
"Be fruitful and multiply, fill the earth and subdue it;
rule over the fish of the sea and the birds of the sky
and over every living thing that moves on Earth."
Passing from its originators,
the idea spread to the far corners of the world.
The mental short-term time horizon of destruction
met with the need for dominion over nature
to secure life from natural disasters and wild beasts.

Oh, how well did we succeed!
The curse of our vital need.
Think and build just for today;
another will come tomorrow, they say.
Whatever we want we want it now,
the future will take care of itself somehow.
We will yet find out this isn't true.
Will we be able to change our paradigm?
Will we give building its rightful due?

The savior who wants to turn men into angels
is as much a hater of human nature as the totalitarian despot
who wants to turn them into puppets.
Eric Hoffer

Catamount

Once more the earlier morning sun
has called me to my favorite boulder,
RikkiCat having her daily run.
Between sips of coffee I close my eyes,
enjoying the precious morning quiet.
A faint noise causes me to look up,
and there, a few feet away,
looking straight at me, sits this puma cat.
There is not threat in her demeanor,
just cautious appraisal by this creature.
I have no fear with this mountain lion so near.
We seem to commune a sense of belonging,
a sense of being one with the world we share.
A squeeze of her eyes, a final goodbye,
and she fades away in the blink of an eye.
Did I imagine her? Was she real?
I truly can't say.

Love is the triumph of imagination over intelligence.
Henry Louis Mencken

Imaginings

More and more, as days go by,
the errors I make multiply,
the body, too, is no longer spry.
After breakfast my RikkiCat waits
to venture to the yard with me.
While she observes, explores her world,
I sit on my favorite boulder,
sipping from my emptying cup.
I watch the dappling of the rising sun,
a light breeze caresses my face.
Closing my eyes, the silence, an embrace.
A gentle tap on my shoulder. I look up,
There, next to me, lo,
stands this ghostly figure telling me softly:
"Come. It is time to go."

There are only two mistakes one can make along the road to truth:
not going all the way, and not starting.
Buddha

Mind's Eye

Here and there flashbacks occur,
some more often, others rare:
The first sight of Victoria Falls.
A summer night in fragrant grass.
The Indian woman assaulted in a bus,
flown to Singapore for treatment, died nevertheless.
A pubescent breast
accidentally to a six-year-old exposed.
The Redwoods on the California coast.
A rocky shore, singing into the wind,
the heads of two women on my thighs reclined.
Olympic eagles cartwheeling in the sky.
Running a business successfully.
The delightful fit with, you know, who was it.
The sting of a first love lost,
knowing that her time now has passed.
The death of a cat pressed close to my chest.
A woman's corpse pulled from the Rhine.
On Sweden's coast an experience divine.
The covert yearning for a certain girl to be mine.

The beauty of Bora Bora isle.
A lion fish snorkeling before my nose.
Picking apples for a dollar an hour.
Planes crashing into towers,
people jumping, trapped by flames.
My sister dying at our place.
Four-leaf clovers Ute could find on request.
The cheese carts after dinner in Burgundy
with the stinkiest goat cheeses tasting best.
Sitting nude in the shallows of the Moorea lagoon
with two Aussies and an NZ woman.
When the captain of our Viscount made it known
that he couldn't get his left landing gear down.
Canoeing across northern lakes.
Running the "wilds" of the Jagsthausen fields.
The death of the nineteen.
Kayaking in Baja was not my take.
Skinny dipping with Sabine in a Georgian Bay.
The guess-who going her independent way.
There's the activity minks are known for.
Running the rapids of the Colorado.
Learning at sixteen to swim on my own
with turds in the polluted Rhine drifting nearby down.

At age six at Barmsee Lake in Bavaria
the wonderful creatures being shown.
As a five-year-old being held three stories high
over the balustrade of a balcony.
Excursions in Utah's Red Rock country.
The explorations in our garden.
In my early teens the run of the neighborhood
without a warden.
These occasional flashes cover almost eighty years.
Of course, there's plenty more.
Uh, oh, some I'd better not reveal.

Always do right.
This will surprise some people and astonish the rest.
Mark Twain

From Shadows to Light

I'd like to close this collection of verse
with a thought on our future
which I hope will be bright.
There will be changes to the better I think,
when we leave the current plenitude
of shadows behind.
Upheaval, pandemic, and realignment
will set the stage for a shining light.
I hope to be able to hang on for a while
to, maybe, see yet a glimmer of a new living style.
And should this hope turn out to be moot
the universe isn't going to give a hoot.

We all feel the chill our present cast on our future.
Nothing less than a global spiritual awakening can transform
us.
What's real must matter more to us than what we wish to
believe.
Albert Einstein

Ten Explorations

The likely Futility of S.E.T.I. Programs.
April 2004

Frank Drake and Carl Sagan suggested that our galaxy might harbor dozens of techno-scientific civilizations. So it may be, but...

Microbial life based on carbon and water may be ubiquitous in the Universe. Even low-level entities may be common. Dinos, or their equivalent, may roam unknown planets, but sentient life is likely to be rare and probably ephemeral, as I will try to show.

The Universe is violent and Nature doesn't care if life is extinguished. The below cited possible upheavals and detrimental conditions are not graded by severity. It must also be understood that the various events and conditions may occur at "inappropriate" times in the evolution of life on a planet and wipe out life forms essential for the rise of sapiens!

Galaxies clash, merge, rip each other apart, which takes hundreds of millions of years. While space is enormously vast, the turbulence created by such an event may, however, affect a viable planet in such systems encounters.

At the center of the Milky Way Galaxy's 200 billion plus stellar population high radiation and gravitational disturbances make stable planetary systems conducive to life unlikely. Multiple star systems, constituting approximately half of all, are unlikely to have planets due to their gravitational and dynamic disturbances.

Factors like these reduce the number of life-supporting stars considerably. With our sun being a G-type star, only F, G and K may have luminosities conducive to water-based life.

218

A supernova event within 50 light years of the solar system would have little effect on microbial life, but serious ones on a techno-scientific civilization.

Planetary Dynamics:

Of the 120 plus extra-solar planets inferred so far all, with the exception of two systems, have planets orbiting their parent star in elongated orbits. Jupiter-size planets need to be sufficiently distant from their sun to allow for inner rocky planets. Elliptical orbits, whether those of an outer gas giant or an inner rocky one, make for unstable orbits. The elongated orbit of an outer gas giant would lead to the eventual ejection of inner rocky planets from the system.

It was once thought that the arrangement of our solar system with its largely circular planetary orbits was also typical for extra-solar systems, but less than 2% of the presently inferred systems seem to be of similar nature.

Neighboring stars may come close to the solar system and jog some Oort Cloud members from their orbits, some of which could spiral inward causing major life-destroying impacts. In 1908 several thousand km^2 of forest in Siberia were leveled by a comet exploding above-ground. Had it taken place a few thousand kilometers westward, parts of Europe would have been leveled!

Comet Shoemaker-Levy breaking up and plowing into Jupiter, drove home the point that an outer gas giant intercepts incoming comets, protecting the inner ones from more frequent impacts. Yet asteroids and smaller space debris cross the orbits of the inner planets. In the course of time their orbits intersect. They then become life killers, sometimes changing the make-up of existing life forms.

The Habitable Zone:

Then there is the "Goldilocks Principle", the not-too-cold, not-too-hot Habitable Zone (HZ) of a stellar system where water remains liquid. Our Sun's luminosity has increased 30% over 4.5 billion years shifting the HZ outward. A lesser luminosity four billion years ago would have required a compensatingly denser atmosphere, a greenhouse effect, to keep water liquid. Today's HZ reaches from just inside Earth orbit to inside that of Mars. A billion years in the future, should the Sun's energy output continue to increase, Earth will orbit outside the Habitable Zone, that is, it will be too hot.

If a G-type star's HZ, due to its mass and composition, is not "just right" at the appropriate time, the evolution of life on a planet may be aborted.

Planet Size or Mass:

A planet within the HZ must be of right size, between 0.5 and 2 Earth masses. A planet with 2G, would require any animal evolved on it to be of very stout built to withstand its gravity with a respective loss of agility. A planet below 0.5 Earth mass could not hold onto its atmosphere. It would also be unable to sustain Plate Tectonics!

Rotational Period:

Jupiter, fastest spinning, rotates in 9.9 h. Its girding storm bands are indicative of little atmospheric north-south exchange.

Our Moon has slowed Earth's rotation over time. It has been calculated that four billion years ago Earth rotated in six hours! A water-rich Earth-size planet with rapid rotation would experience huge storms with little north-south exchange necessary for climate equilibrium. Its oceans would see enormous waves. Its continents would be scoured by continuous winds, reducing the likelihood for the evolution of larger plants. Black Smokers in the ocean depths, or the Earth's interior would provide more favorable locales for microbial life. No Columbus would have crossed the Atlantic if Earth were rotating in 6 hours.

Axial Tilt:

At present Earth's Axial Tilt (AT) is 23.5°. Venus and Jupiter have only minor tilts, thus do not experience seasons. Earth, Mars, Saturn and Neptune have moderate tilts, their poles alternately leaning toward the sun, causing moderate seasons.

Uranus, "lies on its side". Planets maintain their obliquity if not disturbed by outside influences. However, during the formation of a planetary system planetesimals with irregular orbits, may have crashed into other gradually forming planets.

Due to centrifugal forces a rotating planet develops an equatorial bulge. Tidal pull of the Sun, Jupiter and Saturn on this bulge causes the planet's AT to slowly precess, that is, its spin axis slowly slews around like a wobbling top. Earth's precession period is 26,000 years. As a result of this tugging the tilts of all inner planets wobble slightly in complex rhythms. These various influences, taken together, achieve a resonance which may result in dramatic effects.

It is known that Mars has rocked back and forth between 15° and 35° over several thousand years. In the past it has been swinging even wider, up to 60° over

221

tens of millions of years. It may have tipped some 50 times in the past five million years.

When a planet's obliquity approaches a severe inclination, it kind of rolls along in its orbital plane, exposing its poles alternately for half of its year to the sun, leading to severe freezing , then heating of the hemispheres. Seasons would be extreme. While microbial life might survive such conditions, it is unlikely that higher life forms could adapt, certainly no civilization.

Earth-Moon Binary System:

A hypothesis, still under contention, posits that the Moon was created by a Mars-size impactor within the first few hundred million years of planetary formation. The material expelled from Earth aggregated in Earth orbit, some of it falling back, some of it escaped, the majority of the mass, however, coalesced into the Moon. Imagine the huge tides it created, not just on oceans, but also on the then minor land masses.

A smaller impactor would have produced a smaller moon with lesser influence on Earth; a larger impactor might have expelled Earth from its orbit. The impactor had to hit Earth at a "good" angle to produce a "good" obliquity, giving us our moderate seasons. Timing was important; incipient life might have been extinguished or much delayed. No matter how the Moon was created, it stabilizes Earth's AT without which the planet might experience much greater tilts and inclement seasons.

How many such stabilizing systems are likely to exist in the Milky Way!

Heavy Metals:
The formation of metal-rich stars and planets depends on the elemental enrichment of the birth-giving gas cloud. Heavy metals, particularly iron, are prerequisites for life. Iron is fertilizer, food for algae, the carrier of oxygen in mammalian blood. Copper, zinc, manganese, even gold and others are required for metabolic processes. A planet poor in these elements is not a provident place for life. It definitely is not one to give rise to a techno-scientific civilization.

Liquid Iron Core and Magnetic Field:
Earth has a solid inner and a liquid outer core. This does not seem to be the case for Venus and Mars since both planets do not show a magnetic field, which is generated by the friction between the inner solid and outer liquid core.

Aside from its atmosphere, Earth's surface is largely protected from space radiation by its magnetic field. Without an atmosphere and a magnetic field a planet's surface, like that of Mars, becomes sterilized.

A small planet like Mars, cooling more rapidly than a larger one, will see its liquid core solidifying more quickly, causing the loss of a strong magnetic field. Within a few million years the solar wind will then push its atmosphere into space.

A planet's size matters! Too small and it means early curtains for the evolution of life.

Magnetic field reversals do not happen in the blink of an eye but may take hundreds of years. In that time the magnetic pole wanders and field strength lessens causing unknown problems, while the reduced magnetic fields increases mutations.

Plate Tectonics:

A well-placed virgin planet may at first be a water planet with few land masses rising above the waves. Volcanism must then arise to create larger continents. Small Mars experienced some volcanism, but due to its small size and faster cooling its incipient tectonic movement and volcanic activity stopped. Small Mars died early in life!

Once life arises on a planet, Plate Tectonics is essential for the recirculation of carbon concentrated by life and exuded by it into the atmosphere. Without it CO_2 would accumulate producing a greenhouse effect eventually choking all life.

Major flood basalt eruptions occurred in the past, the result of mantle plumes. They are called Trapps, Dutch for steps. The largest, the Siberian Trapps, cover an area the size of Europe and lasted for millions of years. They are implicated in the great Permian Extinction, one of 5 major ones, of 245 million years ago, causing 95% of marine life and 70% of land animals to perish.

The Deccan Trapps were caused when India drifted across where there is nowadays the island of Reunion in the Indian Ocean. This eruption also lasted for millions of years just about 65 million years ago, coincidental with the demise of the dinosaurs, whose coup de grace may have been an asteroid.

The enormous amounts of toxic gases emitted by these eruptions changed the climate. In the case of the Siberian Trapps, once global temperatures rose and oceans warmed, large amounts of frozen methane hydrate, sequestered on ocean floors, were liberated, adding to atmospheric change and temperature.

We do know that enormous quantities of methane hydrate have once again accumulated, waiting for their liberation by our today's progressing greenhouse effect.

The gigantic volcanic Toba eruption on Sumatra 75,000 years ago must have produced a multi-year volcanic winter, severely reducing global human populations.

The Yellowstone caldera erupted several times in the past 1.2 million years and may be due for another cyclical event. This would blanket large parts of the US in layers of ash.

Enormous sub-oceanic slumps similar to one that happened 8,500 years ago off Norway and volcanic island collapses waiting at Las Palmas off the African west coast and as happened in Hawaii, would cause tsunamis of several hundred meter height, washing away entire opposite coast lines. Oceanic impacts of major asteroids would produce similar-size tsunamis. In the past hunter-gatherer societies in unaffected parts of the world kept on going, but today's global civilization is much more vulnerable.

For any of the above events to occur it is likely not a question of "if" but "when".

Change of Global Ocean Currents:

Plate Tectonics moves continents across the globe changing the conveyor belt of globe-girding ocean currents of which the Gulf Stream is a small part. While Continental Drift is extremely slow, giving life time to adjust, present-day warming trends increase the freshwater content of arctic waters and may lead to a retraction of the Gulf Stream. Global warming could cause another ice age. Where would all these northern-dwelling people move to?

Ice Ages:

Ice core records from both polar regions have shown that Earth experienced many ice ages with intermittened warming periods through the past 200,000 years. Many of these changes happened within decades. Only within the past 11,000 years has the climate remained fairly clement, the average global temperature never varying by more than 2° C. Note that our civilizations all arose within this brief time span!

Where would we be, and where will we be, without a stable global climate?

Conclusion:

If the conditions for "life as we know it" are not met, or not at the "right time", or if one or the other of the above "events" happens at the wrong time, low-level life forms may arise and be sustained, but complex life, and techno-scientific civilizations may never arise or be short-lived. Never mind our very own efforts to do ourselves in.

Nature does not seem to care one way or another. Only the tautological Strong Anthropic Principle may protect us. Louis Pasteur supposedly said: "Chance favors the prepared mind". But we need more than just "mind"; we need action.

How many times were the conditions just right to permit techno-scientific civilizations to arise and to survive in our galaxy? Very few – if any!

Snowball Earth
July 2004

In the 1920s the German meteorologist Alfred Wegener introduced the idea of Continental Drift. He primarily based his theory on the apparent fit of the west-African coast with that of South America. Because he did not have a background as a geologist or geophysicist, he did not offer an explanation as to how continents could drift across the face of the Earth. Without substantial evidence, and because no mechanism was known at the time, his ideas were not taken seriously. It would be another 40 years before his idea of continental drift would be accepted. In the early 1960s scientists discovered the mid-Atlantic ridge and its related volcanic activity. It was now possible to measure the plate motion as it pushed crust in both eastward and westward direction from the ridge.

Today science readily accepts the concept of Continental Drift or tectonic plate movement, and the same may likely happen with the hypothesis of "Snowball Earth". Joe Kirschvink of Cal Tech coined the term "Snowball Earth", but like Wegener he did not pursue his idea. Kirschvink was not referring to the "minor" recurring ice ages like the most recent one terminating only 10,000 years ago, but one of entirely different origin. In the 1930s a British geologist presented the outline of a great infra-Cambrian ice age, but he did not have the evidence to support it. Support for his theory did not come forth until the 1980s when a CalTech scientist discovered evidence that ice had reached the equator in Precambrian times. Still, only a few scientists entertained the idea that the entire Earth could have frozen. Most scientist held the opinion that

227

the reflection of sunlight from this global ice sheet would prevent its melting and the Earth would remain a perpetual ice ball. In 1992 Kirschvink countered his opponents with a brilliant solution for this conundrum. He proposed that several major volcanic outbreaks contributed to the melting of the ice sheet! He suggested that this phenomenon could have occurred several times about 700 million years ago. Kirschvink's theory envisions multiple ice advances, extending all the way to the equator, interspersed by periods of volcanic melting.

Why did this happen? Kirschvink suggested that from time to time tectonic plate movement concentrated most of the continents near or at the equator. While located near the poles the darker land masses absorbed a great deal of solar heat and prevented ice from creeping southward. Once land became concentrated nearer the equator, ice slush would have congealed in the polar oceans, eventually forming thicker and thicker sheets. A cloud-free sky with little if any snow fall would have occurred and the average temperature could have dropped to -40° Celsius.

In Iceland, scientists have observed the eruption of sub-glacial volcanoes. As they erupt they release large amounts of CO_2. Carbon dioxide, a greenhouse gas, permits sunlight to enter the atmosphere, but it prevents subsequent infrared radiation from escaping into space. After millions of years the accumulation of CO_2 in the atmosphere produced a rise in the average global temperature initiating a major melting event. Some scientist believe that the melting could have occurred within just a few hundred years. Average temperatures may have soared to +40° Celsius. In addition, frequent hurricanes produced torrential acid rain all over the planet.

To gain support for his theory, Kirschvink mentioned his 'Snowball Earth' idea to Harvard geologist Paul Hoffman who then took up the pursuit. In Namibia, later in many other places where Precambrian rock was exposed, he found a layer of carbonate rock immediately above a thick layer of pebbles and boulders, called drop stones. These drop stones are believed to be glacial till transported by icebergs. After calving from the main ice sheet, icebergs float out to sea and gradually melt, dropping their accumulated till onto the ocean floor. Found immediately above the till deposit is a layer of carbonate rock. Carbonate rocks usually form at the bottom of warm, shallow seas, supporting the idea of either global warming or an equatorial position.

Another possible explanation for this till/carbonate relationship came from a Harvard geologist. He suggested that torrential acid rains fell onto accumulated layers of dust, glacial "rock flour" produced in millions of years of glacial grinding. This dust and acid rain combination was washed into the seas creating, what he described as a fizzing and foaming "Coca Cola" ocean. The dissolved CO_2 dust mixture turned the seas milky white initiating the chemical precipitation that produced the carbonate rock layers found above the "drop stone" layer.

What would have been the effects on life? It is thought that life appeared on Earth within the first 500 million years after its formation. Over the next 3 billion years, mainly single-celled organisms and blue-green algae populated the world's oceans as slimy algal mats, while other extremophile forms could be found in rocks and around underwater thermal vents. Curiously enough, multi-cellular life arose about one billion years ago, not much before the predicted time of the last "Snowball" event. Could there be a connection?

The early Earth's atmosphere was rich in CO_2, but had relatively little oxygen. A large increase in oxygen levels is directly related to the respiration process associated with   life. Oxygen is a basic requirement for animal life. The increased abundance of oxygen in the atmosphere by 550 million years ago could have served as a stimulant for the rise of multi-cellular organisms, cumulating in the Cambrian life explosion. In addition, it is suggested that the nutrients, which enriched the oceans during the "Snowball Earth" periods are thought to have provided food for the rapidly evolving life forms.

The extinction of many life forms in the course of the global glaciations is certain, but some would have survived. Research in Antarctica has shown that light does filter through the top layers of clear glacial ice and through pack ice to the shallow sea bottom. This would permit a certain amount of photosynthesis to take place. Pockets of life would also have persisted near volcanoes on land and near submarine vents to permit the continuation of more basic life forms.

In conclusion, Kirschvink's theory of "Snowball Earth" offers a fascinating addition to the results of tectonic plate movement and its effects on life. Just as the end of the last ice age and the subsequent relatively stable world temperatures made possible the rise of human civilization, so the post-Snowball Earth conditions may have been conducive to the rise of life, the evolution of higher life forms on the planet we know today.

"Snowball Earth: The Story of the Great Global Catastrophe that spawned Life as we know it", by Gabrielle Walker, Ph.D., is a thought-provoking book for additional reading.

Wondrous Water
August 2004

Imagine: If one of the universal constants, the strong nuclear force which holds protons and neutrons together, had been greater by 2% than it actually is, protons would have bound together in pairs. While this state of matter doesn't exist in our universe, had things been different, all protons would have bound up in di-proton nuclei shortly after the Big Bang. One of the protons would have changed into a neutron, the pair becoming deuterium. These deuterium nuclei would then have paired off to form helium the consequence being, that most ordinary matter in the universe would have been helium, not hydrogen. Stars would not have fused hydrogen to helium, nor would water have been produced - the universal solvent.

A solvent is a liquid substance capable of dissolving or dispersing one or more other substances. Water can dissolve more substances than any other solvent. No other substance comes even close to water's capabilities. Nontoxic, water is the carrier of life-giving substances. In fact, only it makes all life possible. While water seems to be chemically simple – it is composed of only two hydrogen atoms wedded to an oxygen atom – it is actually an enormously unusual substance. Yet it is not a reactive one, that is, it does not consume the dissolved substances as other solvents do. And life precisely depends on these unique properties of water.

Galactic water molecules are moving very slowly due to the cold. When two of them meet, they stick together, that is the opposite charges of hydrogen atoms vs. oxygen attract and thus form the weak hydrogen bond. The result is ice.

Yet this attraction, water's hydrogen bonds, keeps water liquid through a wider range of temperature than found for any other molecule of its size. Relatively high heat is required to dissolve multiple hydrogen bonds, that is to convert water to vapor. The evaporation of sweat, a mammalian means of cooling, is accomplished by the amount of heat generated by the body.

Water's thermal parameters are different from other substances. Most compounds contract as they cool and expand on being heated. Water is no different, but only just before it freezes. At $+4°$ C it begins to expand, even when getting colder. By the time it becomes ice, it is actually less dense than liquid water and thus floats instead of sinking. Were this not the case, life on Earth (or elsewhere) would be impossible. If all bodies of water would freeze from the bottom up (if ice were denser than liquid water and would be sinking), no sea or lake-bottom ecologies could survive. Once frozen, bodies of water would remain frozen forever! However, freezing from the top down insulates the water below from further freezing and permits rapid thawing.

If water's density would have been higher, it would have increased the weight of organisms, limiting their size and mobility. A fraction heavier and aquatic life forms would float to the surface; a fraction lighter and they would have sunk to the bottom.

Water can store large amounts of heat, thus the oceans' heat absorbing capacity moderates global climate. Sea temps vary only a third as much as land temperatures. Ocean currents carry and distribute that heat to other areas around the globe. Evaporation from the oceans and other bodies of water produces clouds, which carry their load of water over land areas, precipitating in rain, snow or hail. Where there is no precipitation, there is little if any life. Rivers carry precipitation back to the oceans - and thus it continues - the water cycle.

Water's high surface tension permits it to enter rock crevasses. Since it expands on freezing it breaks rocks apart, frees from them and nearly dissolves all known chemicals to at least a minimal extent. It distributes these diverse chemicals through the environment, of which more than 33 can be found in the oceans. The process dissolving rocks produces soil, without which no plant life would be possible, thus no agriculture. Its high surface tension draws water up through the soil within reach of plant roots and from there up immense trunks to leaves and even the needles of the giant *Sequoia sempervirens*.

Its low viscosity, one of the lowest of any fluid, enables it to penetrate and carry nutrients through cell walls. Had water a higher viscosity, circulatory systems as we know them, could not have evolved. If its viscosity were higher, no microorganisms, cells or fishes would be able to swim through this more viscous medium.

Diffusion rates in water are very short, but only over short distances, enabling oxygen and nutrients to diffuse to cells in a capillary system extremely quickly – but only because water's viscosity is so low. This enables small organisms to ingest nutrients and discharge waste by diffusion. Both make for efficient metabolisms. Without these two characteristics larger or higher life forms would be impossible. We, a "higher" life form, virtually depend on this multitude of microorganisms!

Isn't it wondrous that 70% water, some carbon and a few trace elements can make a human being, and with slight variations, all of life.

The Probability for Intelligent Life in the Universe.

A critical look at present assumptions for intelligent Life.
May 2005

Current successful attempts to locate other planetary systems, the presence of amino acids in meteorites, the possibility that they might even contain microbial fossils, and the likelihood of water on early Mars, have supposedly increased the probability that life may be common across the Milky Way galaxy. This idea is nowadays widely mentioned in the media and scientific publications. But what kind of life would it be – microbial life, scurrying creatures, dinosaurs, a Mesopotomian-like culture, or a techno-scientific civilization that we could communicate with?

This critique will be anthropocentric. It is based on our definition of life, that is on carbon and water, not on science-fiction fantasies. Yet caution is called for. Did we not assume that other planetary systems, once found, would be similar to our nicely ordered solar system? So far, only two of the 130+ inferred giant extra-solar planets appear to have orbits resembling Jupiter's and Saturn's, whereas all others have highly elliptical orbits or orbits too close to the parent star, leaving no room for rocky, Earth-type planets. And with that finding, we get to the crux of the matter. So, let's start with the basics.

The probability for extraterrestrial life is reduced by the following:

The high radiation environment at a galaxy's center and the gravitational disturbances due to the proximity of stars are not conducive to sustain carbon and water based creatures. The older, metal-poor stars in the bulge and the globular clusters of the halo are also less likely to support life. Metals and heavier elements are essential for life.

At least half of all solar systems consist of binaries or multiple stars, which would eject any protoplanets due to the gravitational disturbances of the multiple suns.

Only F-, G- and K-type stars have the luminosity, neither too hot nor too cold, to create a habitable zone within which a rocky planet could maintain liquid water, a prerequisite for life. These stars are also richer in metals and heavier elements, which make them likelier to have rocky planets. O-, B- and A-type stars, hot-burning giants, which are rich in hydrogen and helium, appear to be unsuited to offer a viable environment for life. M- and C-types, while metal-rich, lack the requisite luminosity. These criteria further reduce the number of life-supporting systems.

A gas giant, like Jupiter, seems to be required to intercept comets or asteroids coming in from the system's outer reaches to reduce the impact frequency on other planets in that solar system, which can severely impact the survivability of even low-level life forms on those planets. This gas giant must also have a circular orbit, so as not to eject inner rocky planets due to the gravitational disturbance it produces.

That only a very few of the so far observed extrasolar planets have circular orbits may be an artifact of our current limited observation methods. However, with agreement among astronomers, that the inner reaches of a protoplanetary disk contain insufficient material to form Jupiter-size planets, then large-size planets found orbiting close to their parent star must have been accreted farther out and then wandered inward.

Such large planets collect material to clean out a ring-like gap in the disk, whose inner part revolves faster than the outer one. This difference in speed transfers angular momentum outward, resulting in the inner part of the disk and the giant planet to lose energy and to drift inward, in the process preventing the accretion and establishment of Earth-like inner-system planets.

Elliptical orbits only increase the instability of a system. As long as we have no satisfactory explanation as to how the relatively stable circular orbits of our own solar system can evolve and find similar ones, we must assume that non-stable systems are the more prevalent, reducing the likelihood for planetary systems conducive to life.

To be habitable, a rocky planet must lie within a sun's Goldilocks zone, not too hot, not too cold, where water remains liquid. If none lies within, there will be no life!

If a planet is too large, its gravity would stymie the growth of all living entities and reduce the agility of mobile creatures.

If a planet is too small, its liquid-iron core would solidify rapidly, with plate-tectonics stillborn. Volcanism, caused by plate-tectonics, replenishes atmospheric gases. Without this, the solar wind would blow the planet's atmosphere into space within a few millions of years. This is what happened to Mars.

A planet's rotational axis must be roughly at a 90° angle to its orbit to experience clement seasons. Should its obliquity be strongly inclined, it would roll-along in its orbit, experiencing extreme climate swings of half-year freezes and half-year boils for its hemispheres.

A newborn planet is likely to rotate rapidly. The young Earth's rotational period was calculated to have been six hours. The immense storms and wave action generated on such a planet would have made the development of life on its surface precarious, if not impossible. The rapid rotation would prevent the exchange of temperature, between the equatorial regions and the poles (as shown by Jupiter's bands).

We know that Mars has changed its obliquity many times through millions of years, at times up to 60°. This is primarily due to Jupiter's gravitational influences, but also to that of the sun and other planets. Most of all, it is due to the lack of a substantial moon like Earth's. The Earth-Moon system is actually a binary planet system. The large Moon stabilizes Earth's axis, preventing it from tipping. If the impact theory of the Moon having been created by a Mars-size body hitting the early, still liquid Earth, is correct, then such a scenario of Right Time, Right Mass, Right Angle, etc. is not likely to be repeated many times across the galaxy. The large Moon, too, has slowed Earth's rotation to our current more tolerable 24 hours.

Computer simulations seem to indicate that the larger the outlying gas giant, the greater the water accumulation on inner rocky planets. Thus, a gas planet, substantially larger than Jupiter might provide for an inner, mostly ocean-covered planet. Octopuses and other sea creatures would not invent fire.

Time is of the essence – that is, eons of time are necessary. For over three billion years, Earth held nothing more than single-celled organisms. More complex life is less than 570 million years old.

Cataclysms, like volcanic lava flows lasting for millions of years, giant methane-hydrate releases, the eruption of super-volcanoes (e.g. Toba), major asteroid impacts, and complete freeze-overs of the planet, caused enormous extinction events in the past. What if their timing in the evolution of life had been different on Earth? What if one of these events occurred again? A supernova within a distance of 50 light years might cause only mutations in microbial life, but would most likely severely affect a techno-scientific civilization.

Are conditions elsewhere in the galaxy conducive to the evolution of an upright walking ape, or a creature of different but similar design? Would it develop manipulative organs, similar to hands? Would its social arrangements promote an increase in brain size? What means of communication would it evolve?

Human civilization arose only after the cessation of the last ice age 11,000 years ago. Since then, the stable global temperature, never varying more than 2° C, has made agriculture possible.

Is it likely that cultures like ancient China, Persia, Rome, etc. could have evolved into a techno-scientic civilization? What are the social and philosophical requirements to make this possible? Of the various earthly cultures, only one accomplished this — Western civilization.

Various natural catastrophes could put an end to, or at least severely crimp a global techno-scientific civilization. Examples are asteroid impacts, failure of an equivalent of the Golf Stream, the release of methane-hydrate gas, super-tsunamis caused by island-volcano collapses, ecological deterioration, and last not least, war. So, the Universe may teem with microbial life, but — taking all the above influences together — the probability for Intelligent Life is infinitesimally small. And to be sure, more than a Plato or Archimedes are required to make a techno-scientific civilization! Proponents of life-in-the-universe have suggested that the rise of intelligence is inevitable. But did they take into account that, despite the plenitude of stars, the likelihood of all the favorable conditions coming together in the right sequence is highly unlikely?

A Personal View of Existentialism
December 2005

This is a talk I gave in my friend's, Dieter Schuring's class, at the Osher Learning Institute during the fourth semester 2005.

Some of what I'm going to talk about transpired already in prior communications with Dieter. Some of my information came from as far as Denmark and Germany.

To some extent this will be a personal account, that is my encounter with existentialism on a direct, personal basis, now being affirmed by what I'm learning in this class. I've headlined my talk:

A Call to Battle and a Fight until Death.

Why a Call to Battle and why a Fight until Death?

Existence precedes the essence of being human, meaning that we enter the world (Heidegger's Thrown-In) and must subsequently define ourselves. It is regarded as particular and individual, an avenue to the meaning of being and a challenge to choice.

To be authentic, to have a lucid consciousness that life is indeed meaningless, and yet commit oneself through active choice.

The dangers lurking in the apparent COSMIC meaninglessness of life can result in nihilism (existence is senseless & useless/social organization so bad as to destroy it) and alienation, that is the feeling of powerlessness, meaninglessness, formlessness, cultural estrangement, social isolation and self-estrangement.

242

This vacuum calls to be filled by passionate commitment to establish, to grow INDIVIDUAL meaning, to evolve and define oneself throughout life.

This is the Call to Battle – for it is no small task!

And since life's definition ought not to end – with death yet to be defined – it is also a Fight until Death.

To people of active religious faith some meaning of one's life may be defined by the respective doctrine. Yet even they must struggle with the vagaries of life, such as the persistence of evil and the effects of natural catastrophes.

The Danish religious philosopher Soren Kierkegaard expressed this battle with doubt, the meaning provided by his faith, by his words: "Trods det", "trotzdem" in German, "in spite of" in English. While I am no member of a religious faith, but an agnostic, I use Kierkegaards's "trods det" in a secular sense as my Call to Battle – "in spite of" of the universe's apparent meaninglessness and vagaries, I must persevere and strive.

Throughout our lives life tests us and we must deal with these recurring tests, make our choices and take responsibility for them.

A few weeks ago I sent the below words to Dieter:

This is why Buddha advised leaving all desires behind,

for all else would end in suffering.
But as I've said before, and now here again:
I am by Intellect Western Man.
We must strive!
If I suffer, so be it!
In the process I learn and, hopefully, grow wiser.
I shall also overcome.

243

And if not, then so be it!
I must accept impermanence.

Every human being is possibility, meaning freedom. He is never what he was, but always what he will be. He is, will be, what he makes himself! And this freedom makes him responsible to himself, which no church, no party, nor any leader can take in its place.

Man is nothing but a draft, an outline. He exists only to the extent to which he realizes himself that is, he is nothing else but the totality of his actions, his deeds.

And by discovering himself he discovers also others and discovers them as the condition for his existence. Yet this interdependence and societal feedback impinging on his being calls in turn on his freedom which has been called: "Overcoming the socially given."

The ethical rigor of existentialism is thought to produce anxiety, fear of assuming existential responsibility, fear of freedom. The result can be the flight from freedom into anonymity, enabling the denial of responsibility.

As a teenager my question was: What do I live for? I must have been 17 when I arrived at my answer: To live life and make the best of it. Sounds simplistic, right? But I have followed this admonition to the present. Not long thereafter I took official leave from the Lutheran Church.

But then the question arose: By what rule shall I live that life? And my answer was: To protect and further life, but to terminate it also when I deemed it necessary. This I have also done.

I consider myself the product of Christian Culture, but I am no Christian. My ethics are my own. I have made mistakes and will likely make a few more before my demise.

Except for the war experiences of my childhood, I, together with many of my generation, have lived / are living during one of the most, if not the most comfortable period in all of human life. I mention this, because most of us in the Western World have had no need to grub for our existence. The question therefore is, how we, how my approach to deal with the world, to explain it, would stand up if conditions would not be so favorable. Would I still overcome? Nothing to say even about the ultimate question – that of death.

When the ultimate question, that of my own death arises, I do not, cannot know, how that will be. It will be the ultimate test of the totality of my meaning. Will I be able to stick to it when the time comes?

This is why I am a man of the present, not the beyond. May I end my talk with Kipling's final stanza of his poem IF which, in its entirety, I see as pure existentialism:

... If you can fill the unforgiving minute with 60 seconds worth of distance run, yours is the Earth and everything that's in it.

And – which is more – you'll be a man my son!

We, every one of us, must create ourselves, must work and sometimes battle for what it means to live, even if our lives are ever so short, so ephemeral.

Thank you very much.

Tsunami
The History, Causes, Effects, and Types of this Phenomenon.
December 2007

Horrific images of death and destruction from the Indian Ocean tsunami of December 26, 2004 were broadcast around the world within hours of the incident. People saw first-hand the destructive power of these giant waves and the large loss of life that occurred throughout the region. However, most people do not understand what is taking place during a tsunami. For one thing, the tsunami came without warning. Some, ignorant of its warning signs, were actually drawn closer to watch the surging waves. Often sea level recedes prior to the surge, exposing the nearshore environment and stranding sea life. Local people, unfamiliar with this exciting event, may even venture out to collect stranded fish. Obviously, shoreline dwellers as well as visiting landlubbers need to be educated about tsunamis, for it may save their lives one day.

Tsunami, is a Japanese word meaning 'harbor wave'. Such sudden surges were often observed within harbors. Due to the high frequency of earthquakes in Japan, the Japanese were one of the first trying to understand this phenomenon.

Unfortunately, this is not the case with many other cultures living along shorelines. Due to the relative infrequency of tsunamis, most potentially affected people have no experience in dealing with them. The occasional local tsunami is often unknown at distant locales. Even the memory of a past destructive tsunami fades with time and subsequent generations live without the knowledge of their danger.

The greatest danger from a tsunami is a lack of warning time. In the early 1960's, a tsunami warning system was established in Hawaii by UNESCO's IOC for the Pacific Ocean region. Once an earthquake is being recorded, the center informs countries around the Pacific Rim about a potential tsunami hazard. Following the 2004 Indian Ocean tsunami such a network was also established for this region. However, such systems are not fail-safe due to many variables that affect the reliability of the network. Due to the high number of earthquakes occurring, a tsunami warning may not be issued every time, for, if it turns out to be false, people may loose confidence in future reports. Then there is the cost. Many poorer countries do not have the means for evacuations, or a country's warning system may not be operative.

Almost all tsunamis are caused by some form of tectonic movement. Its three causes are: Sudden pressure release of subducting crustal plates, flank failure of submarine slopes, and flank failure on mountains above sea level. The displacement of earth materials caused by these events can be in the hundreds of cubic kilometers. Each of these displacements produce a like displacement of water – becoming the tsunami, made visible once the traveling energy reaches shore.

The 1964 Alaskan earthquake displaced about 500 km^3 of rock, while the 1960 Chilean event displaced a huge 1,500 km^3! Each such displacement produces a like displacement of water – becoming the tsunami. The most devastating tsunamis originate from subsidence or uplift of the ocean floor. Examples include Sumatra, Indonesia (2004), 230,000 deaths; Messina, Italy (1908), 90,000, and Lisbon, Portugal (1755), with 100,000 earthquake & tsunami deaths. Smaller events touched Hilo, Hawaii, swamped by the Chilean (1960) tsunami. Crescent City, CA, experienced a one meter surge from the 1964 Alaska event.

Above surface flank failure like at Letuya Bay, Alaska (1958), produced a giant splash reaching a height of 520 m. Being a sparsely populated area, few deaths resulted. Occasionally, island volcanoes like Krakatoa, Indonesia, (1883) erupt. It produced a tsunami of up to 37 m in height. Along the shores of nearby islands over 30,000 people lost their lives. Krakatoa's offspring, Anak Krakatoa, is growing again and it, too, may someday explode causing even greater losses due to the shoreline's increased population. The volcanic eruption on the Island of Thera (Santorini) about 1490 BC destroyed most of the island and its culture.

Other events include face collapse on volcanic islands (Hawaii, 1868/1975). Smaller ones may not be as destructive, and affect a relatively small region. However, there is evidence of late Holocene Hawaiian flank failures, whose effects were felt as far as the southeast coast of Australia. On Molokai and Lanai paleo marine conglomerates have been found at 170 m above today's sea level. It is thought that they were deposited by the flank failure of a nearby island and the resulting local tsunami.

Evidence for massive flank failures, none of which have occurred in historic times, has been found on the ocean floor surrounding the Hawaiian islands, Reunion in the Indian Ocean, La Palma in the Atlantic, and elsewhere. While the likelihood for one of these catastrophic events to happen soon is low, some must be expected in the more distant future.

Submarine flank failures can occur on many earthquake-prone coast lines and on sea mounts. Such debris avalanches happen on unstable coastal scarps. Being proximal to coasts, they permit little, if any, warning time of impending tsunamis to local populations. Evidence for such events in historic and prehistoric times exists for the Oregon and California coasts. While tsunami height at these locations is unlikely to exceed 10m, losses in today's times would be substantial. Other submarine landslides have happened on New Guinea (1998), and the Balearic Islands (2003).

Shifts of rock material cause a like displacement in the volume of water. The resulting change in water level on the open ocean may vary at most 2 m from the surrounding wave action, and may not even be noticeable. The speed of a tsunami depends upon the depth where the displacement occurred: the deeper the event, the faster the rate of travel. The 1960 Chilean earthquake generated tsunami wave speeds of up to 900km/h. While tsunami waves can travel around the globe, their effects diminish with distance, reaching their minimum amplitude (height) after 12,000 km and there may raise water levels by only a meter.

Wave motion is not water flow, but a flow of energy. The medium (water) itself does not travel. Ocean waves at the interface between air and water are called orbital waves. They have a length from crest to crest of up to 400 m and travel at speeds between 25 to 90 km/h, whereas tsunami wave lengths are in excess of 200 km. When such a surge reaches shore its length shortens. The onrushing water column is forced upward by the shallow shore, producing the tsunami surge. Such waves generally max out at 15 m, however, heights of 30 m (Okashiri, Japan, 1993), and (Ceylon,

2004) have been reported. Tsunami wave period on the open ocean is up to 90 minutes, but with increasing speed near shore, crests shorten to 10-45 minutes. Tsunami surges are usually repetitive and subsequent wave surges are often higher than the first one(s). A common misconception is that oncoming tsunami waves are always indicated by a retreat of the water from shore. If a crest reaches shore first, it leads to an immediate surge of water! It is only because of the extremely long wave lengths of tsunamis and their long troughs, that retreats are observed more often than surges.

Beyond the three major tectonic causes a least likely, but eventually to be expected event, is the ocean impact of a large asteroid, which could cause a tsunami of several hundred meters in height. The Yucatan impact 65 million years ago with its resulting tsunami and other effects, appears to have caused a major extinction. Tsunamis of varying magnitude will continue to happen roughly every five years around our 'living' globe. Some will produce horrific results, yet most will see only minor loss of life – a footnote in the lives of millions – but a terrifying and deadly experience for those directly exposed.

Pragmatism
December 2013

"What's Pragmatism? Does it work on my smart-phone? What will it do for me?" you may ask.

Well, as a first step: If you engage an app, a search engine on your smart-phone, entering "pragmatism," you will get a definition. Old-fashioned as I am, I googled it and here's the shortest one I found:

"A practical, matter-of-fact way of approaching or assessing situations or of solving problems."

You may now think: What the heck? Of course that's how things get done! But this assumes we are rational beings, which we are not! Our prime motivator is emotion, with beliefs founded on emotion! And beliefs need not be of a religious nature. Oh no, we find plenty of "belief" in the scientific endeavor. A scientist may hold dear a theory he has worked on for ages and has great difficulty letting go of, even when facts argue against it.

Whenever we face a problem, what is necessary to tackle it is the engagement of "ratio," reason. But to put aside our emotional engagement on the subject in order to concentrate on how to solve the problem and to engage Pragmatism, is no easy task!

Permit me now a brief introduction to the originators of Pragmatism.

Since Classical Greek and Roman times, there have been prominent philosophers, such as the Greeks: Epicurus, Democritus, and Plato; the Romans: Pliny, Plutarch, and Cicero; the Germans: Kant, Hegel, and Nietzsche; and the French: Descartes and Sartre. While each of these men, together with their many other 'seekers,' contributed to the human font of knowledge, the most notable American philosophy (philosophy

251

meaning 'Love of Wisdom'), typifying the American mind, is Pragmatism – meaning to have a penchant for the practical.

The originators of Pragmatism in the second half of the 19th century were Charles Peirce, William James, and John Dewey.

To quote Raymond Pfeiffer on the subject in *Philosophy Now*:

"Pragmatism was originally the thesis that the meaning of an idea can be found by attention to its practical consequences. Such an idea is no mere penchant for the practical: Rather, it is a direct and specific theory of meaning with implications beyond the laboratory and the library."

And further:

"Pragmatism was one way he (Peirce) applied logic and the methodology of science to philosophy. His theory of knowledge was *fallibilist*, breaking with much of the philosophical tradition and maintaining that some beliefs are true, some not, but that no knowledge is infallible, and that there is no certainty."

Pfeiffer quotes William James as saying:

"(He) maintained that the practical needs of humans in this world might justify beliefs and practices that cannot otherwise be proven true. The faith of our fathers and mothers might be reasonable not because it is true, but because it is practical."

Dewey is said to have "viewed the old philosophical search for real, final truths as a threat rather than a virtue. It is the search for knowledge that emerges from the junk heap of human thought and misguided prophets. Whatever promotes thinking, dialogue and rational inquiry should be encouraged, and whatever stifles it avoided."

252

To list some of the best characteristics of American Pragmatism as stated by Pfeiffer:

a. "The extent to which an idea fulfills important human goals, clarifies the idea and also provides evidence for and against the likelihood of its truth.

b. Sharp, fixed distinctions of thought and reality are not reflected in nature, where one thing fades off into the next, one flows into the other and the complexity of our thought is clarified only by theories that give tentative illumination to reality."

And, last not least, c. "Whatever promotes reasoned dialogue, inquiry and further understanding is good, and what stifles it is bad."

Are we now getting closer to an answer to the third question asked initially: What will Pragmatism do for me?

Sadly, as we observe the political goings-on on the national level, we can say that American Pragmatism has gone by the wayside! On a personal level: What is bullying in schools to accomplish, based on irrationality and emotions. Does it solve any problem? Does it promote well-being?

Allow me to close on a personal note. On a cursory level I became acquainted with Pragmatism decades ago when I still lived in Germany. While I did not know anything of its originators and its deeper meanings, the practical applications, and their American origin held a profound attraction for me, and in a small way contributed to my settling in the United States of America.

So, some time ago, I wrote a poem in which I expressed my sentiment on the subject, calling it:

253

Pragmatism
Once, many, many years ago
I came across this magic word,
so plain and yet so real.
It stayed with me throughout my life,
had import and appeal.
And without delving into it,
it was my guiding light
to find solutions, how to deal,
with all of life's contingencies.
Be practical, find out what works,
and if it doesn't, change your tack.
Thus did I work, not all was swell,
but in the end, lo and behold,
much that I did worked out quite well.

And, not to forget, Pragmatism implies the application of tolerance, for without tolerance we will be unable to find solutions to the problems we are facing.

Nelson Mandela, while coming close to being a saint, was first and foremost a supreme pragmatist.

Forty Billion
Potentially Habitable Planets
A Rebuttal
December 2013

What we, as humans, consider "habitable" must mean habitability for oxygen-breathing, land-based animal life, not only microbial life.

A continuing question is how many planets may orbit the estimated 200 billion stars in the Milky Way Galaxy, and how many of those could support life as we know it? For scientists – but hardly for the general population – it is an important question whether or not life is common in the universe.

Our current level of observation of star systems, while impressive, is broadly confined to inference, statistics and guesswork. But more precise data are certain to become available in the future.

At present, we know of only one form of life, that found on Earth, based on the presence of water and carbon. The precursors of proteins based on these elements have been found in certain meteorites, but whether other elemental combinations exist to create a form of life remains unknown. We can only proceed by what we know and by its probability. Wishful thinking ought not let us be carried away by exaggerating probabilities – while also not underestimating them.

NASA's Kepler space telescope has identified about 150,000 stars in the constellation Cygnus – this in a miniscule field of the galaxy – of which 3,000 stars showed a temporary lessening of brightness from which the transit of a planetary body was inferred. The size of such transiting planets, whether of Earth-size or gas giant, is still approximate.

An independent study of 42,000 stars, similar to our Sun or slightly cooler and smaller, indicated over 600 potential planets, of which, however, only 10 were approximately Earth-size. Since only a fraction of planets, as seen from Earth, are orbiting their stars face-on, the team used statistics to determine that about 22 percent of all Sun-like stars have Earth-size planets in their habitable zone.

Based on these latest studies, NASA's Ames Research Center proposed that the Milky Way Galaxy is populated by "Forty Billion Potentially Habitable Planets," a report that was widely published by the media with plenty of hype, yet without critical evaluation of the probability. Again, humanity's wishful thinking of finding other life beyond ours in the universe ran amuck.

What is not considered in this estimate is that the galactic center, packed with radiation-emitting stars, is inimical to life, while the outer regions of the galaxy are poor in heavier elements necessary for the accretion of planets and the rise of life. Approximately one-third of all star systems are binaries or multiple systems, whose gravitational complexity make stable orbits for planets minimal. The majority of stars are smaller than our Sun, being called M-type stars. Their habitable zone is therefore located farther inward. While these smaller stars have longer life times, any purported planets need orbit closer in, being in danger of becoming tidally locked, with one hemisphere always facing the sun, the other experiencing galactic cold, a situation not conducive for the development of life.

A G-type star's luminosity increases through its lifetime, making its habitable zone not only space-dependent but also temporary. A planet at one time within the habitable zone may eventually find its conditions for life diminished, and vice versa. And for life to develop takes time, several billions of years, first for ocean-dwelling life to produce oxygen, where it at first was protected from UV radiation. Once ocean-dwelling life has generated enough oxygen to bind the free iron, oxygen can be released into the atmosphere where it can generate ozone, protecting future land-based life from UV radiation. And a star only 1.5 times the size of our Sun will see its habitable zone move rapidly outward, leaving less time for the development of life.

So, let us address now in greater detail the probability for the rise of extraterrestrial life. Before entering into the gist of the matter, let's consider some side issues which, nevertheless, affect the rise and maintenance of life. If comets truly provided all of Earth's water, it may have also happened elsewhere. However, what if a water-world arose, which without the initiation of plate tectonics (because of small size, too small an iron core, insufficient radioactive elements to generate heat) remained a globe-spanning water world? Another inhibiting factor could be long-duration glaciations, or even "snowball" episodes covering the entire planet in ice sheets.

Finally, here is a listing of conditions required to coalesce for habitability – beyond the mere extrapolation of the number of star systems with planets.

1. R = low Radiation environment. We can likely exclude the great number of stars located in and around the galactic core, inimical to life.
2. G = G-type star

3. B = Binary or multiple star systems make up approx. 1/3 of all stars. Their gravitational pull makes planetary orbits rare or unstable

4. C = Carbon and other elements required for life in a system's composition, provided by dust clouds, novae, etc.

5. I = Iron-nickel core for magnetosphere, protecting life from radiation.

6. S = Size of planet, not too small, not too big, exerting gravity on possible life forms.

7. P = Plate tectonics to generate volcanism and a first primitive atmosphere.

8. D = Distance from star to be within the Goldilocks' zone where water remains liquid.

9. T = axial Tilt. If too great, seasons would be extreme.

10. O = circular Orbit. An orbit carrying the planet outside the Goldilock's zone would result in periodic, severe glaciation

11. P = regular Planetary system, as found in ours as opposed to most, at this time inferred extraterrestrial systems that are often hugely chaotic.

12. J = no Jupiter-size giant nearby which would exert gravitational influence and disturb the putative planet's orbit and axial tilt over time.

13. M = a substantial Moon to stabilize the axial tilt of the parent planet. If Earth's Moon was truly created by the early impact of a Mars-size body, the question arises how often such an event would take place in the galaxy at the proper time?

In 1961 Dr. Frank Drake suggested a formula by which he attempted to calculate the probability for extraterrestrial intelligent civilizations by entering assumed values for his various parameters.

Here is another formula which uses the above parameters 1-13 to guess the probability of finding habitable planets:

$$H = R \times G \times B \times C \times I \times S \times P \times D \times T \times O \times P \times J \times M$$

$$H = .5 \times .5 \times .1 \times .8 \times .6 \times .8 \times .5 \times .8 \times .9 \times .5 \times .2 \times .6 \times .1 = 0.000020736$$

which, multiplied by the putative 40 billion means, maybe, 830,000 habitable planets.

From it we may conclude the unlikelihood of finding life or animal-habitable planets in our neighborhood, much less that ET will contact us. So much for the all-too-casual claim that the Milky Way Galaxy harbors up to 40 billion potentially habitable planets. There could be a lot of them, but perhaps 40,000 times less than claimed!

For additional information see the book "Rare Earth" by Peter D. Ward and Donald Brownlee. My own amendments in 2019 is that numerous additional parameters are required.

Exceptionalism
A Historical Analogy
May 2014

Exceptionalism is the idea that one nation is different from the norm, such as the United States of America, as expressed by her philosophical stance, her system of government, her economic system, her social order, even her geography. Since Alexis de Tocqueville's first use it has become a staple of American elites, especially of conservatives. They hold that America is unique and superior to virtually all other nations and is also largely self-sufficient.

Let us consider an analogy:

Between 1405 and 1433 the Chinese Emperor Yongle dispatched seven maritime expeditions under the command of Admiral Zheng He to India and the East African coast, displaying the flag, but returning with little to show for the expenditure. His successor Emperor Hongxi determined that these expeditions had been wasteful. The giant sailing ships were decommissioned, only smaller vessels were allowed to be built, and maritime trade was restricted to the near environs.

During the 15th century into the 1800s China generated the greatest portion of the world's GDP, making her the wealthiest nation on Earth. Self-sufficient, her requirements were satisfied internally and by near-abroad trade. Her emperors and elites considered their nation the greatest, justifiably so – exceptional when compared to all others in science, technology, commerce, and social organization.

In the year 1498, only a few decades after the Chinese discontinued their maritime quest, the

Portuguese explorer Vasco da Gama landed in Calicut on the west coast of India. Had he met Admiral Zheng He's armada, his small Portuguese carracks, three- or four-masted sailing ships, would have appeared like rowboats to the huge vessels of the Chinese.

Yet it did not take long, once the sea route had become known, for many of these small European vessels to appear in the Indian Ocean, and then the Indonesian islands. The wealth of spices lured them on – first the Portuguese, followed by the Spanish, the Dutch, British, and French. Not long thereafter their ships arrived at the Chinese coast seeking to trade for the riches of China. Much later, in 1854, the American Commodore Perry's Black Ships opened up Japan to trade with the West. By the late 1800s China had become a toy of the Western nations, having ceded various coastal territories.

The science and technology of the West had surpassed the wealth and organization of the Chinese Empire. Western expansionism, including that of the United States, established numerous colonies across the globe. Eventually, Europe, then the USA, produced the majority of the world's GDP.

Fast forward:

After World War II the victorious USA dominated the seas and world affairs. In a mighty effort she launched multiple manned expeditions, e.g. the Apollo Program, to the Moon. The U.S. succeeded magnificently, out-competing the Soviets. But nothing of commercial value was brought back from the Moon, and President Nixon canceled the Apollo program because of its high cost. Further manned space expeditions were from then on confined to the near environs, Earth orbit, their product the so-called International Space Station.

Manned space exploration beyond near Earth orbit was deemed too expensive. The funds saved were needed to finance the social programs of a democracy and benefited the country's elites. Whether private efforts to rekindle manned space exploration will be successful remains to be seen.

America was largely self-sufficient with plenty of resources, and now dominated the world order, especially after the demise of the Soviet Union. Conservative political circles   basked in American "exceptionalism" – justified by her Constitution – but in reality no longer justifiably so. The U.S. was becoming intertwined in world trade. Needs that could no longer be satisfied at home were now being met from abroad.

In 1950, the U.S. merchant fleet accounted for 43% of world shipping trade. By 1995 this had shrunk to 4%! Today, it is the Asian nations' vessels – Chinese, Taiwanese, Korean, Japanese – that ply the oceans and bring their goods, often cheap, to the shores of the United States, in return collecting the wealth and the obligations of the receiving country. The situation very much resembles the earlier Chinese-European trade, although it is in reverse direction. So far no war ships have arrived.

In Africa and South America, China is leasing or buying up land for the production of her agricultural needs and the extraction of mineral resources. These land acquisitions are not colonies but . . .

Of course, the carrier fleets of the USA still patrol the oceans, keep the sea lanes open, and project power. Nothing equivalent of this nature was done by the China of the 1500s. But the Chinese and Indians are building their own carriers now. How much longer will America's superiority last, considering changing technology which may well make current carriers vulnerable?

And how many engineers and scientists is China graduating compared to the United States?!

No analogy is ever exact but there are some disturbing similarities, despite the 500 years difference, with one thing in common: Both great nations in their time, China and the United States, rightly thought themselves to be exceptional – until their exceptionalism came to an end. Both rested on their laurels, and wound up being surpassed by upstarts.

Analogies can be instructive!

December 26, 1776
March 2017

It was a fateful morning when General George Washington crossed the ice-covered Delaware River!

He surprised Britain's Hessian auxiliaries under the command of Johann Rall, hired out to the British by their various German princelings. Not all of these troops were Hessians, only the majority, and the American Revolutionary War was not the only time Hessians fought for foreign powers. For the British it was cheaper to pay for these auxiliaries than to recruit their own soldiers. The Americans called them "mercenaries" to emphasize their foreign status, and offered them land to encourage desertion.

As it happened, the Hessian soldiers had celebrated Christmas, which did not pass without substantial alcoholic rations having been dispensed the day before, the 25th of December, Christmas Day. Of course, these libations had helped put most of the men into sleep.

Washington had crossed the ice-covered Delaware in early morning. The attack near Trenton was a rout with few casualties, but resulted in many prisoners, almost two-thirds of the enemy army, who now had to be ferried across the river together with the military hardware that had been captured. Stores of rum had also been plundered, with some of the celebrating victors becoming drunk and needing to be pulled from the icy waters. In the days to come several more crossings ensued, followed by more defeats of British troops, before Washington retreated to winter quarters opposite Trenton.

It was a hard winter, with enlisted men being discharged to return to their families, and others deserting. The war raged back and forth. In the infamous winter of 1777-78 at Valley Forge, the Prussian officer, Baron von Steuben, helped to improve the discipline of the Continental Army.

Carl Schurz, another German-born American, became Brigadier General, serving with distinction. Independence was achieved on January 14, 1784 when Congress signed the peace treaty. Schurz, now a politician, was known for his high principles and is remembered for saying: "My country, right or wrong; if right, to be kept right; and if wrong, to be set right." His wife Margarethe was instrumental in establishing the kindergarten system in the United States.

Sixty-four years later, in 1848, when much of Europe was in turmoil, the German-American artist, Emanuel Gottlieb Leutze, thought of creating the oil-on-canvas painting "Washington Crossing the Delaware," commemorating Washington's accomplishment. He also saw it as a stimulus for the German liberal awakening, a movement against the established powers, which, however, succeeded in squashing the uprising. This led to the exodus of many men to America, most trying to evade the draft.

As a child, Leutze had moved with his parents to America, but had returned to Duesseldorf, Germany, in 1841, where he enrolled in the Koenigliche Kunstakademie, eventually becoming a professor. At the time Duesseldorf was a venue for other American painters. He loved to convince some, as well as visiting American tourists, to sit for him in the creation of the painting's characters.

Being fine art, the painting is not accurate in many respects. Leutze used the Rhine River as his back-drop, which is broader than the Delaware. The ice flows would have been sheet-like, not as crystalline as depicted, and Washington would likely not have stood in the tippy boat. But what does all this matter? It is the heroic image Leutze depicted and glorified, which appealed to so many, as is shown by the numerous copies made of this picture.

The group of people manning the boat is representative of the mix of the American population. There's a Black man and an Indian; there's General Greene and the young James Monroe, as well as a blanket-covered farmer.

Leutze finished his first painting in 1850, but it was soon damaged by fire. Restored, it was purchased by the Kunsthalle Bremen, where, in 1942, it was destroyed in a bombing raid by the British Air Force. Leutze had painted a copy of his original work which was exhibited in New York in 1851, where it was viewed by tens of thousands of people. It was purchased at a substantial sum for the period, and after changing hands several times, was finally donated to the Metropolitan Museum of Art before the turn of the century.

Numerous copies were painted. One such copy hangs in the West Wing of the White House. This iconic painting is one of the best known historical images of the American Revolutionary War.

September 2019   Photo by Elke

Made in the USA
Monee, IL
25 August 2020